GIFTED GAMES™

NNAT® TEST PREP
for the NNAT2® / NNAT3® Level C

Gateway Gifted Resources™
www.GatewayGifted.com

PLEASE LEAVE US A REVIEW!

Thank you for selecting this book. We are a family-owned publishing company - a consortium of educators, book designers, illustrators, parents, and kid-testers.

We would be thrilled if you left us a quick review on the website where you purchased this book!

The Gateway Gifted Resources™ Team
www.GatewayGifted.com

TABLE OF CONTENTS

INTRODUCTION

INTRODUCTION

ABOUT THIS BOOK ---

This book helps prepare young learners for taking the NNAT2® / NNAT3® Level C.

THIS BOOK HAS 5 PARTS:

1. Introduction (p. 4-9):
- About This Book
- About The NNAT2® / NNAT3®
- Practice Test Notes
- Test-Taking Tips
- The Kids' Detective Agency

The Kids' Detective Agency

To increase child engagement and to add an incentive to complete book exercises, a detective theme accompanies this book. Read page 9 ("The Kids' Detective Agency") together with your child. The book's characters belong to a detective agency. They want your child to help them solve "puzzles" (the exercises in the book) so that your child can join the detective agency, too! After your child completes the book, (s)he will "join" the Kids' Detective Agency. However, feel free to modify as you see fit the number of pages/exercises your child must complete in order to receive his/her certificate. (The certificate for you to complete with your child's name is on page 96.)

2. Warm Up Activities (p. 10-17)

Be sure go through these together with your child before starting the Practice Tests! These basic examples provide valuable explanations/tips for tackling the four NNAT® Level C question types.

3. Practice Test 1, Practice Test 2, and Practice Test 3 (p. 18-92)

The three practice tests included in this book provide:
- an opportunity to build critical thinking and problem solving skills
- an opportunity to practice focusing on a group of questions for a longer time period
- a way for parents to identify points of strength and weakness among the test question types

These practice tests are meant to help children develop critical thinking and test-taking skills. A "score" (a percentile rank) cannot be obtained from these. (See page 6 for more on gifted test scoring.)

4. Answer Keys for Practice Tests (p. 93-95)

These pages provide answer keys for the practice tests. They contain additional brief explanations for most of the questions . (They also include the directions, should your child need you to read the directions to him/her again.)

5. Afterword (p. 96)

Information on additional books and your child's certificate

A NOTE ON FILLING IN "BUBBLES"

Your child may or may not have to fill in "bubbles" (the circles) to indicate answer choices. Check with your testing site regarding its "bubble" use. We have included "bubbles" in this publication to distinguish the answer choices.

Show him/her the "bubbles" under the answer choices. Show your child how to fill in the bubble to indicate his/her answer choice. If your child needs to change his/her answer, (s)he should erase the original mark and fill in the new choice.

A NOTE ON THE QUESTIONS

Because each child has different cognitive abilities, the questions in this book are at varied skill levels. The exercises may or may not require a great deal of parental guidance to complete, depending on your child's ability.

We suggest showing your child the example questions starting on page 10 (the Warm Up Activities) as a brief introduction before (s)he attempts to complete a practice test. Make sure there is not any confusion about what the questions are asking the child to do.

Unless your child is already familiar with the NNAT2® / NNAT3® question format (through completion of other test prep materials or other gifted tests), we suggest completing the first practice test together.

WHAT YOU NEED
- This NNAT® TEST PREP book
- Pencil and eraser for your child

ABOUT THE NNAT2® / NNAT3® ----------------------------------

Gifted tests, like the NNAT2® / NNAT3®, assess a child's cognitive abilities, reasoning skills, and problem-solving aptitude. NNAT® stands for Naglieri Nonverbal Ability Test®. As a "non-verbal" test, this test does not require test-takers to listen to multiple question prompts, nor does it assess verbal comprehension or verbal skills. Testing procedures vary by school / program. These tests may be given individually or in a small group environment, by a teacher or other testing examiner. These tests may be used as the single determinant for admission to a selective school or to a school's gifted program. However, some schools/programs use these tests in combination with individual IQ tests administered by psychologists or as part of a student "portfolio." Other schools use them together with tests like Iowa Assessments™ to measure academic achievement. See the next page for more information on test sections. **Check with your testing site to determine its specific testing procedures.**

Here is a general summary of the scoring process for multiple-choice standardized gifted tests. **Please check with your school/program for its specific scoring and admissions requirements.** First, your child's raw score is established. The raw score equals the number of questions your daughter/son correctly answered. Points are not deducted for questions answered incorrectly. Next, this score is compared to other test-takers of his/her same age group using various indices to then calculate your child's percentile rank. If your child achieved the percentile rank of 98%, then (s)he scored as well as or better than 98% of test-takers in his/her age group. In general, most gifted programs only accept top performers of *at least* 98% or *higher*. Please note that a percentile rank "score" cannot be obtained from our practice material. This material has not been given to a large enough sample of test-takers to develop any kind of base score necessary for accurate percentile rank calculations.

NNAT2® / NNAT3®

- The design of these two tests is **very** similar.
- Both consist of 48 questions.
- Both last approximately 30 minutes.
- Both have the same four question types (see p. 10 for detailed explanations of these):
    - Pattern Completion
    - Reasoning by Analogy
    - Spatial Visualization
    - Serial Reasoning
- Both tests' questions consist of shapes, lines, and figures.
- In the NNAT2®, test questions' colors could be blue, yellow, white, and black.
- In the NNAT3®, test questions' colors could be blue, yellow, white, black, and green.

PRACTICE TEST NOTES

PRACTICE TEST COMPOSITION

- This book consists of three practice tests, with 50 questions each.
- Each of the three practice tests contains the four NNAT® Level C question types: Pattern Completion, Reasoning by Analogy, Spatial Visualization, and Serial Reasoning.

- Pattern Completion (14 questions); #1 - #14 in each test
  p. 18-24 of Practice Test 1; p. 43-49 of Practice Test 2; p. 68-74 of Practice Test 3
- Reasoning by Analogy (16 questions); #15 - #30 in each test
  p. 25-32 of Practice Test 1; p. 50-57 of Practice Test 2; p. 75-82 of Practice Test 3
- Spatial Visualization (5 questions); #31 - #35 in each test
  p. 33-35 of Practice Test 1; p. 58-60 of Practice Test 2; p. 83-85 of Practice Test 3
- Serial Reasoning (15 questions); #36 - #50 in each test
  p. 35-42 of Practice Test 1; p. 60-67 of Practice Test 2; p. 85-92 of Practice Test 3

QUESTION TYPE COMPOSITION

- This book contains a range of difficulty levels to accommodate the varying degrees of cognitive levels and testing experience of children who would use this book.
- The first few questions in each section (Pattern Completion, Reasoning by Analogy, Spatial Visualization, Serial Reasoning) of each practice test begin with relatively simple questions.
- Your child may find these first few questions fairly easy, depending on his/her cognitive skills and his/her experience with these types of questions.

PRACTICE TEST ANSWER KEYS

This section, on p. 93-95, contains:

- Directions (If your child needs additional guidance on how to answer questions, read these aloud.)
- Answers (Tally the number answered correctly/incorrectly for an overview of your child's strengths / challenges as they pertain to test question type.)
- Explanations (These briefly explain the correct answers.)

ADDITIONAL PRACTICE

WWW.GATEWAYGIFTED.COM

- We offer another NNAT® Level A/B book, available at www.GatewayGifted.com and Amazon.com®.
- We offer a FREE e-book with 40+ gifted test prep questions, go to: www.GatewayGifted.com for yours.

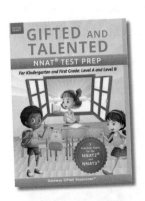

TEST-TAKING TIPS

Tips For Answering Questions

✓ **Do not rush.** Look carefully at the question and <u>each</u> answer choice.

✓ **Use process of elimination.** You receive points for the number of correct answers. You will not lose points for incorrect answers. Instead of leaving a question unanswered, at least guess. First, eliminate any answers that are obviously not correct. Then, guess from those remaining.

✓ **Double check.** Before marking your answer, double check it by going through the question and answer to make sure it makes sense.

Common Sense Tips

✓ **Make sure your child gets enough sleep.** This one is so obvious, yet so important. Studies have shown a link between not getting enough sleep and children performing below grade level and scoring lower on tests.

✓ **Make sure your child eats a breakfast for sustained energy and concentration.** Complex carbohydrates and protein are the best choices - avoid foods/drinks high in sugar.

✓ **Use the restroom prior to the test.** The administrator may not allow a break during the test.

✓ **Don't get overly stressed.** Children pick up a lot from adults. Even though the gifted testing process can be stressful for adults, try not to let your child get worried. Instead your child should focus on doing his/her best. The test will have challenging questions, and sometimes, (s)he will simply not know the answer. When this happens, instead of worrying, tell him/her to remain focused on answering the question the best (s)he can and use the process of elimination (outlined above).

THE KIDS' DETECTIVE AGENCY *(Read this page with your child.)*

Alex

Sophie

Freddie

Max

May

Anya

We're the Kids' Detective Agency. We need another member to join our detective agency. We think YOU have what it takes!

"What does a detective do?" you may ask. Well, a detective figures out puzzles, solves problems, and finds answers to questions.

To prove you're ready to join us, you'll put your skills to the test in this book. Together with your mom, dad or other adult, you need to solve puzzles. The adult helping you will explain what to do, so listen carefully!

A good detective:

- Pays attention and listens closely
- Looks carefully at all choices before answering a question
- Keeps trying even if some questions are hard

Your parent (or other adult) will tell you which questions to do. After finishing them all, you will become a member! (Remember, it's more important to answer the questions the right way than to try to finish them really fast.) After you're done, you'll get your very own detective certificate.

When you're ready to start the puzzles, write your name here: _____

The below "warm up activities" will help you and your child better understand the four question types on the NNAT® Level C. Do these together with your child. The simple examples and brief explanations serve as an introduction to these four question types including hints for how to best answer them. The book's three Practice Tests are organized by these four question types.

QUESTION TYPE 1: PATTERN COMPLETION

Which answer goes in the place of the white box with the question mark to complete the "puzzle"?

1.

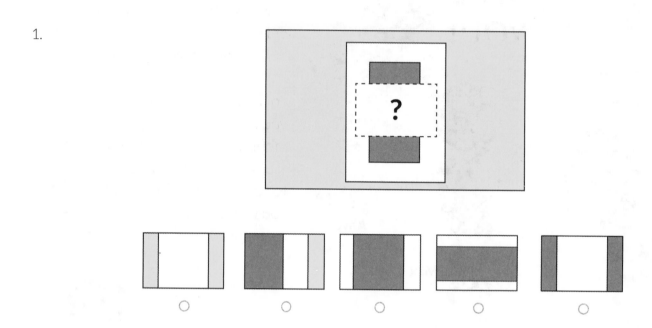

Directions for all Pattern Completion questions: Here is a puzzle where a piece is missing. (Point to the box that has the question mark.) Which one of the answer choices (point to the row of answer choices) would go here? (Point to the box that has the question mark again.)

First, look closely at the pattern's elements: the lines, colors, shapes, and any other figures. Then, do the same with the area around the white box. How do the elements look next to the white box with the question mark? Examine things like color, length, width, and quantity. Finally, figure out how the "puzzle" would look like underneath the white box, if the white box could be picked up. (The answer is C.)

Be sure that you look at the overall picture (or pattern). Some questions will require you to look beyond the area touching the white box and at the pattern presented in the overall picture as well. See the examples on the next page.

The first one involves a pattern of blue triangles and their changing sizes. The triangle size increases from left to right. Look at the pattern of increasing size in the row above and the row below the white box. (The answer is B.)

2.

3.

Look at how the yellow arrow rotates. Across the row, from left to right, it rotates approximately 45° counterclockwise. Look at this rotation pattern from left to right in the row above and the row below the white box. (Answer is C.)

4.

Look at the pattern that the yellow shapes make around the larger white shape. In this example, you should also look at how the green and white sections look next to the white box. (Answer is B.)

QUESTION TYPE 2: REASONING BY ANALOGY

Here, your child selects the answer to go in place of the question mark to complete the analogy. Questions contain geometric figures. Your child will determine how the figures change across the rows.

To help your child understand Reasoning by Analogy questions, this wording may be helpful: *"(Point to the top left box.) This changes to this. (Point to the top right box.) Then, (point to the bottom left box) this would change to (point to the box with the question mark) __. We need to figure out what would go here."* You could also use wording that is common for all analogy questions (not only in NNAT® analogies). *" (Point to the top left box.) This is to that. (Point to the top right box.) As this (point to the bottom left box) is to (point to the box with the question mark) ___. We need to figure out what would go here."*

Sometimes, analogy questions have one "change," while others have more than one "change." Examples 1-14 have one "change." Example 15 has two "changes." Common "changes" are in these examples.

1. Color Change
(Answer is E.)

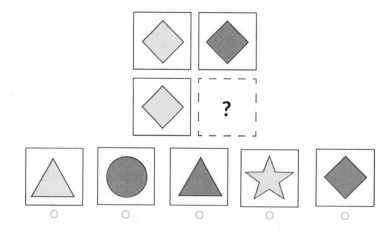

2. "Flip" / Mirror Image

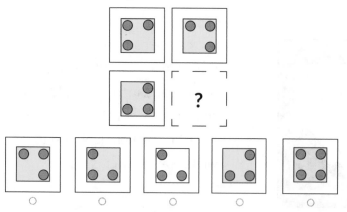

Comparing the left box to the right box, the left box "flips." The second box (the right box) is a mirror image of the first box (the left box). (Answer is B.)

3. Rotation

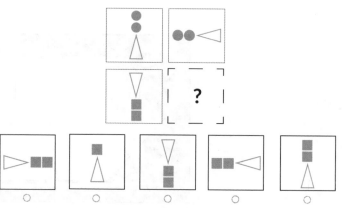

The figure inside the box rotates 90 degrees counterclockwise. In future questions, be sure to pay attention to the degree of rotation (i.e., 45, 90, or 180 degrees) <u>and</u> the direction of rotation (i.e., clockwise vs. counterclockwise). (Answer is A.)

4. Size Change (Answer is D.)

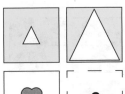

5. Shape Change ("This > That"; on the bottom row, the reverse) (Answer is B.)

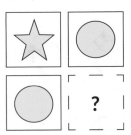

6. Color Reversal (Answer is A.)

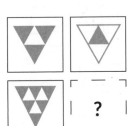

7. Add/ Remove Figures (here, 1 is added) (Answer is C.)

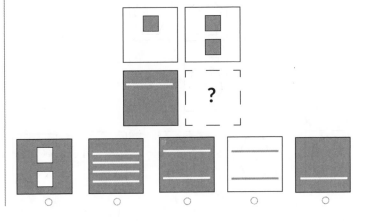

8. Same (No Change) (Answer is D.)

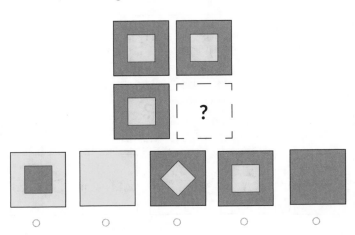

9. Whole to Half (Answer is C.)

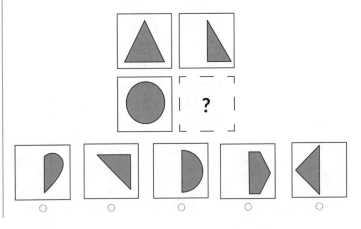

10. Rotation, Example #2 (Example #1 is on p. 12)
The dark quarter moves clockwise 1 quarter. (Answer is B.)

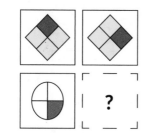

11. "Flip" / Mirror Image, Example #2
(Example #1 is on p. 12) (Answer is A.)

12. Number of Sides Change
The number of shape sides increases by 1. (Answer is E.)

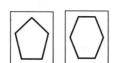

13. "Flip" / Mirror Image, Example #3 (Example #2 is above; Example #1 is on p.12) (Answer is E.)

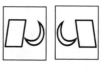

14. Color Change / "This color becomes that color."
Here, blue becomes yellow, white becomes blue, and yellow becomes white. (Answer is E.)

15. Two Changes: Flips and Changes Color
The figure rotates 90° counterclockwise and the 2 smaller shapes become blue. (Answer is A.)

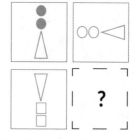

QUESTION TYPE 3: SPATIAL VISUALIZATION

Spatial Visualization questions usually have three pictures per row. Frequently, the questions require your child to figure out how the first two boxes on the bottom row would appear if they were "combined" in a third box. Your child should look carefully at the row above to figure out how the boxes "come together" in the third box. Sometimes across the row, your child must recognize how the objects have rotated within the box or "flipped" (similar to what occurs in Reasoning by Analogy questions). With simple Spatial Visualization questions, when the first 2 pictures combine, there is no additional change (meaning that the elements simply combine). However, in more challenging questions, the elements in the third box not only combine, but they also rotate, "flip" in, or they change in some other form.

1. The first 2 pictures combine.
(Answer is E.)

2. The first 2 pictures combine.
The shapes "flip" in to the box.
(Answer is B.)

3. In the second box, the shapes "flip" in to the box. In the third box, they "flip" to the box's other sides (left to right/ right to left). The first choice is the only choice showing the 2 triangles from the second box, both having moved from left to right/ right to left.
(Answer is A.)

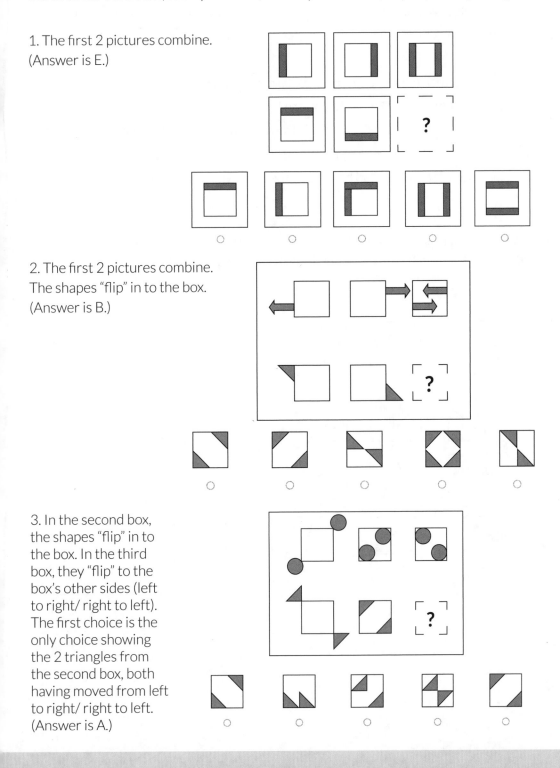

QUESTION TYPE 4: SERIAL REASONING

Serial Reasoning questions have similar elements and require similar problem solving skills as Reasoning by Analogy. However, they are arranged on a 3 x 3 (9-box) matrix. To find the answer, your child must closely examine how the elements in each box change across the rows and down the columns.

It is important that your child does not rush through these. The answers can be easily missed at first.

1- Have your child look carefully at the top row. Can (s)he find a pattern?

2- Have your child look carefully at the middle row. Can (s)he find a pattern similar to the one found in the top row?

3- Have your child look carefully at the bottom row. What would go in the empty box to complete the pattern?

If (s)he does not find a pattern across the rows, then (s)he should try to find a pattern down the columns.

1- Have your child look carefully at the first column. Can (s)he find a pattern?

2- Have your child look carefully at the second column. Can (s)he find a pattern similar to the first column?

3- Have your child look carefully at the last column. What would go in the empty box to complete the pattern?

Here, each row/column has either a heart, star or trapezoid and has one shape filled with either dots, vertical lines or is plain.

The examples here list common themes present in Serial Reasoning questions. If you haven't already, be sure to go through the examples/themes listed in the Reasoning by Analogy questions starting on page 12.

1. Shape Type / Shape Design
(Answer is E.)

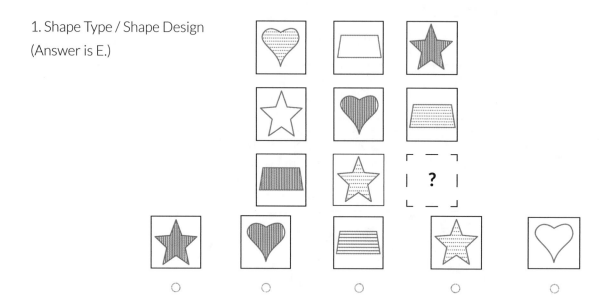

2. Shape Quantity
(Answer C.)

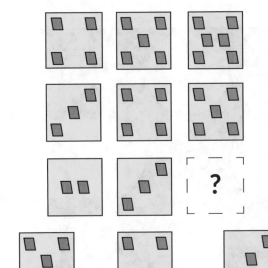

3. Combined Elements
Elements in first box are "broken apart" in the second and third box, across the rows. Down the columns the elements in the first two boxes "combine" in the third box.
(Answer is B.)

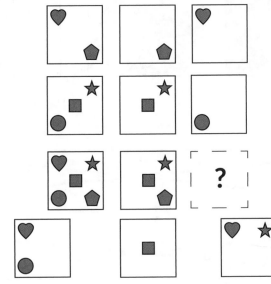

4. Position Change
(Here, the position of a smaller object changes within the larger figure.) Across the rows the star moves clockwise around the group of circles. Note that the color of the circles remains the same across the row. (Answer C.)

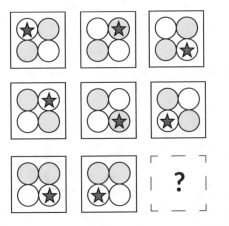

1

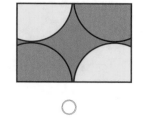   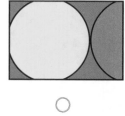   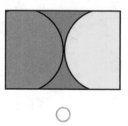   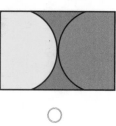   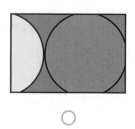

○   ○   ○   ○   ○

2

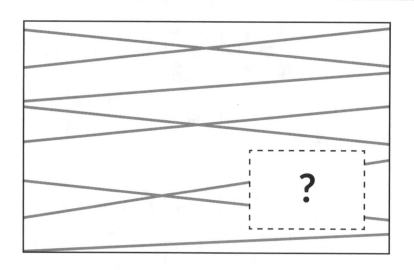

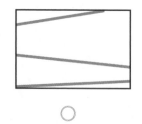   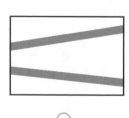   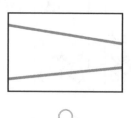   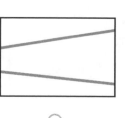   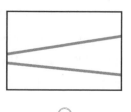

○   ○   ○   ○   ○

3

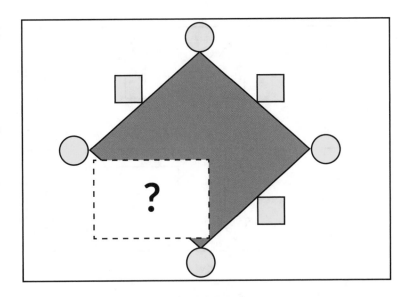

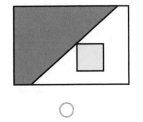 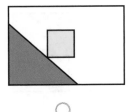 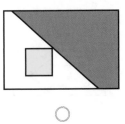 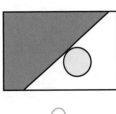 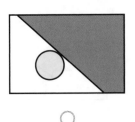

○ ○ ○ ○ ○

4

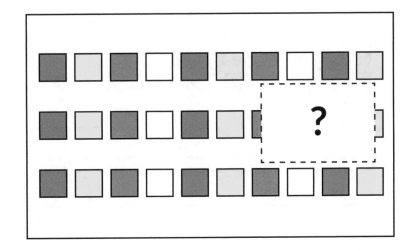

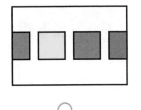 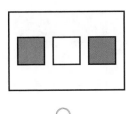 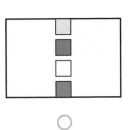 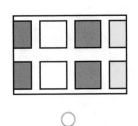 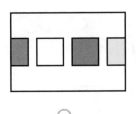

○ ○ ○ ○ ○

5

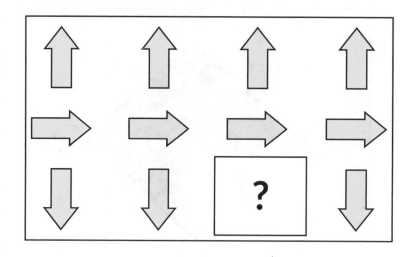

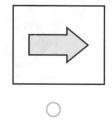 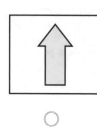 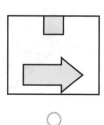 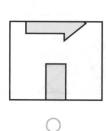 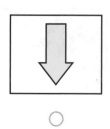

○   ○   ○   ○   ○

6

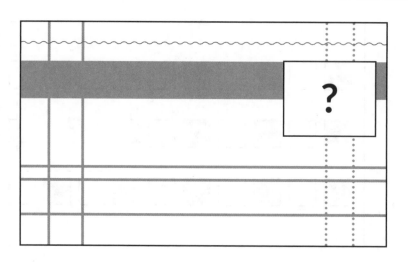

 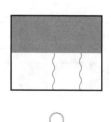 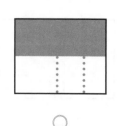 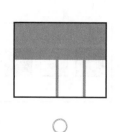 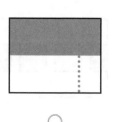

○   ○   ○   ○   ○

7

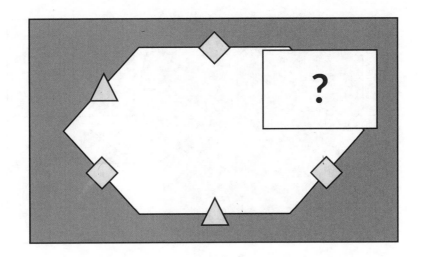

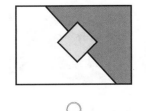   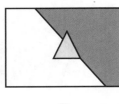   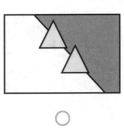   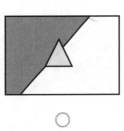   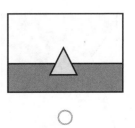

○   ○   ○   ○   ○

8

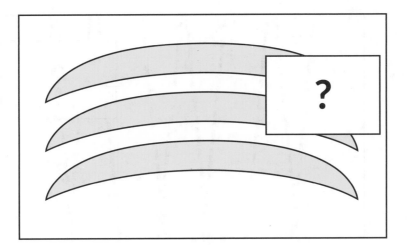

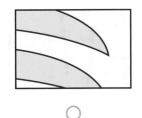   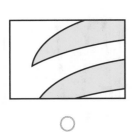   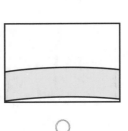   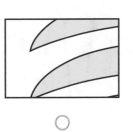   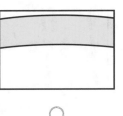

○   ○   ○   ○   ○

9

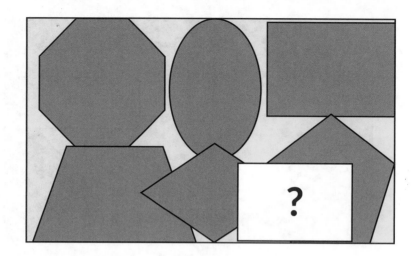

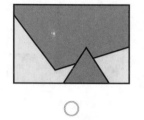 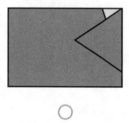 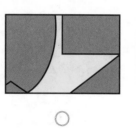 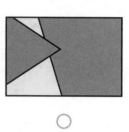 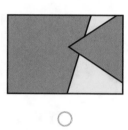

○   ○   ○   ○   ○

10

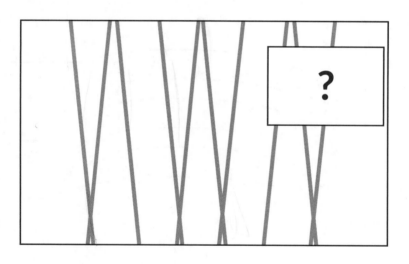

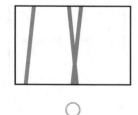 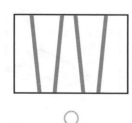 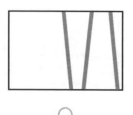 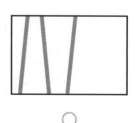 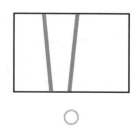

○   ○   ○   ○   ○

11

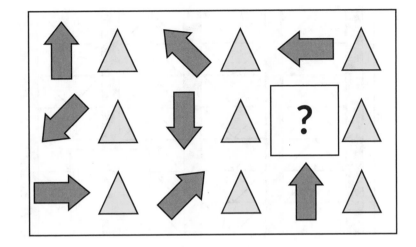

○ ○ ○ ○ ○

12

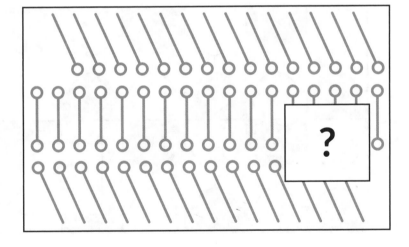

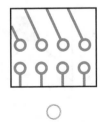

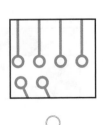

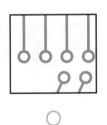

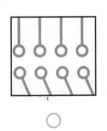

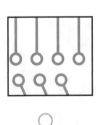

○ ○ ○ ○ ○

13

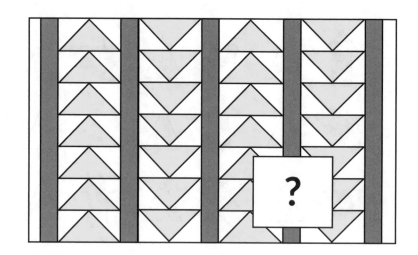

　　　　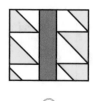

○　　○　　○　　○　　○

14

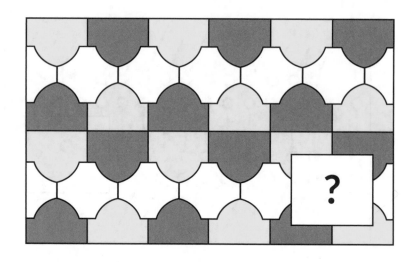

　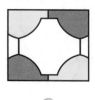　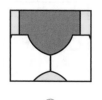　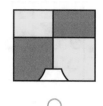　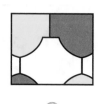

○　　○　　○　　○　　○

15

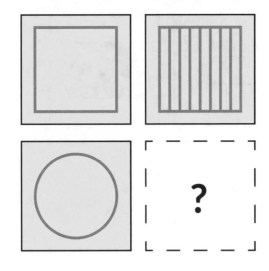

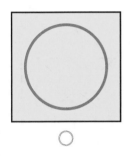 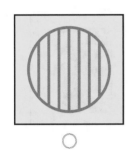  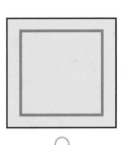 

16

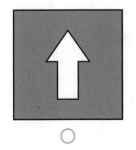    

17

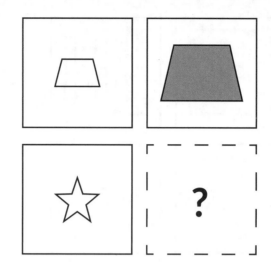

 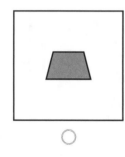  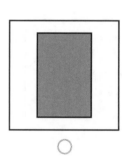 

18

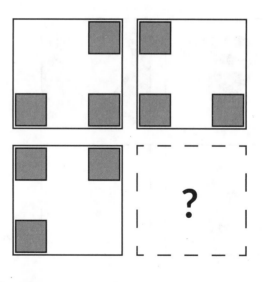

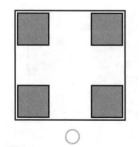 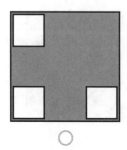 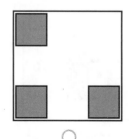 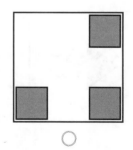 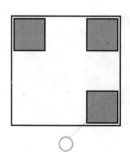

19

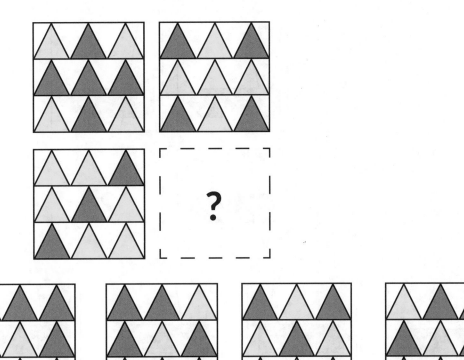

20

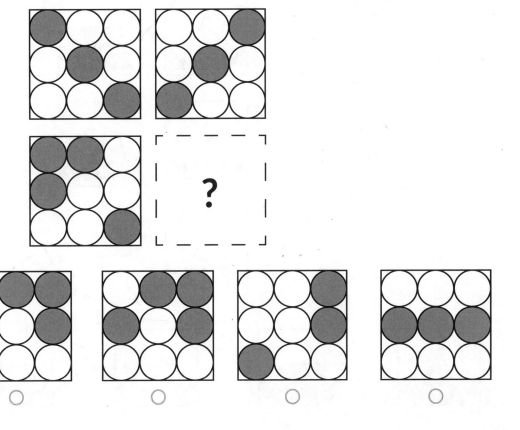

21

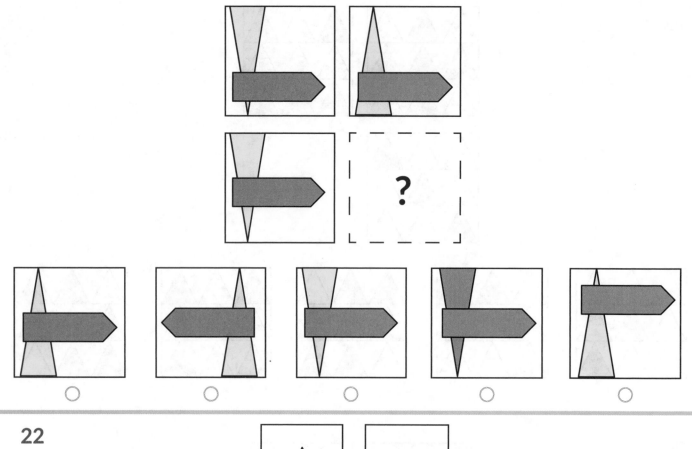

○   ○   ○   ○   ○

22

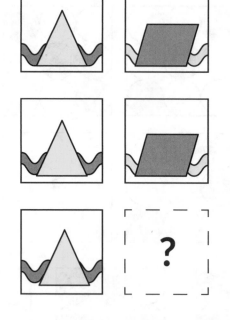

      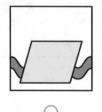   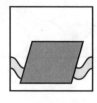   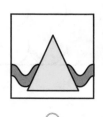

○   ○   ○   ○   ○

23

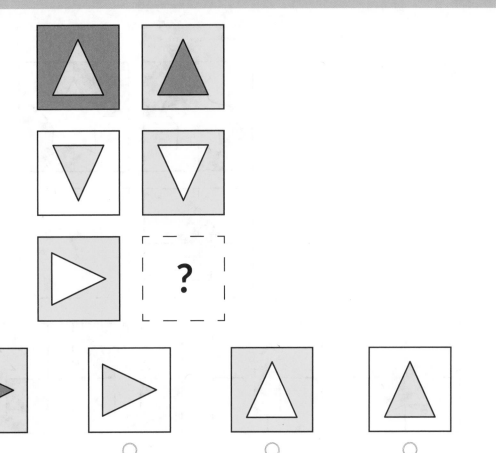

24

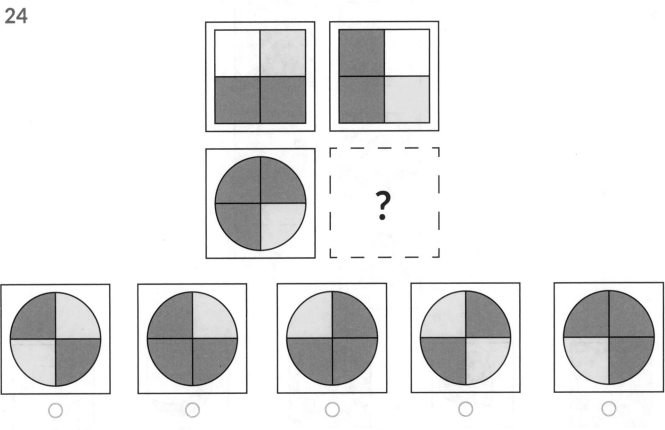

25

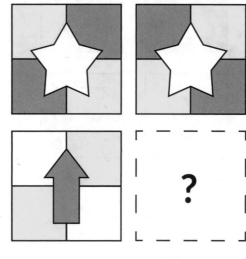

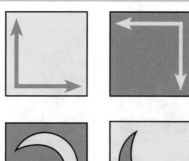

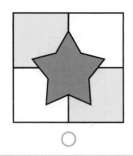   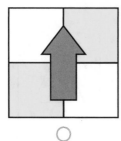   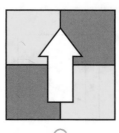   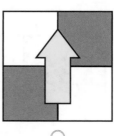   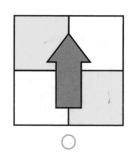

○   ○   ○   ○   ○

26

   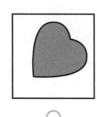         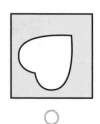

○   ○   ○   ○   ○

27

28

29

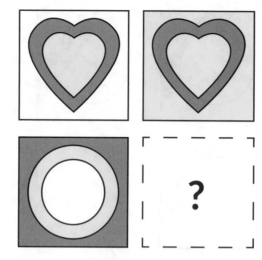

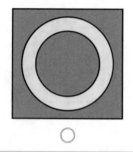
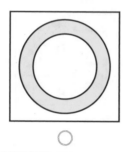

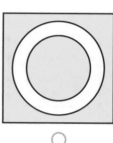
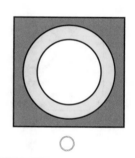

○   ○   ○   ○   ○

30

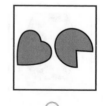

○   ○   ○   ○   ○

31

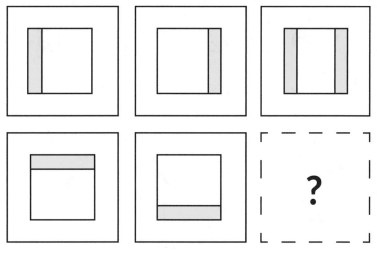

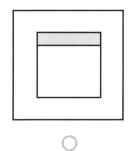

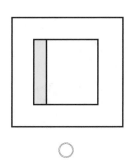

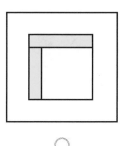

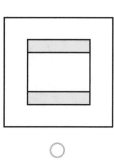

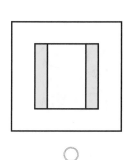

○　　　○　　　○　　　○　　　○

32

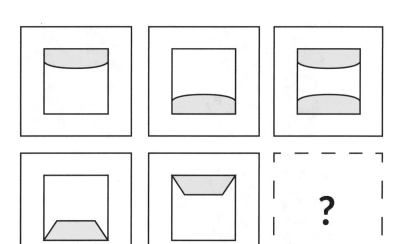

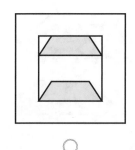

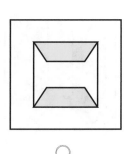

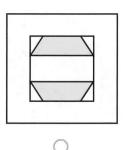

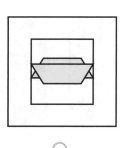

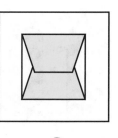

○　　　○　　　○　　　○　　　○

33

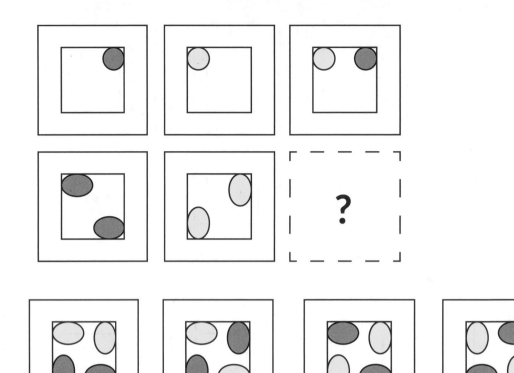

○   ○   ○   ○   ○

34

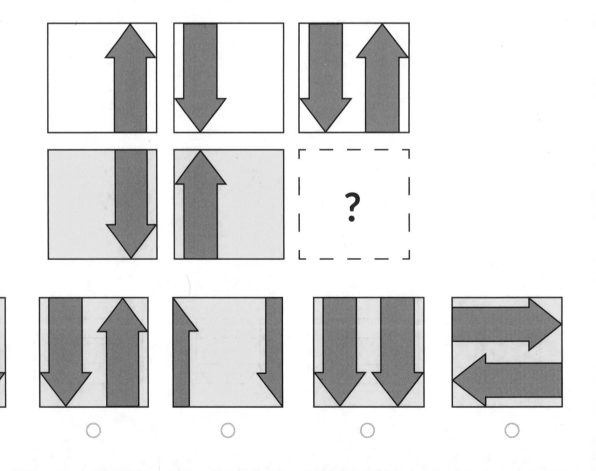

○   ○   ○   ○   ○

35

36

37

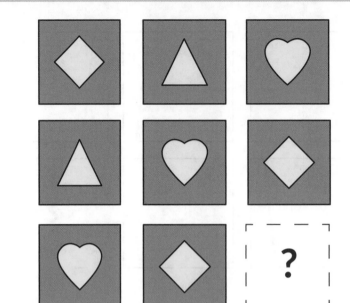

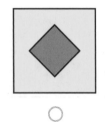
○

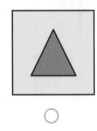
○

○

○

○

38

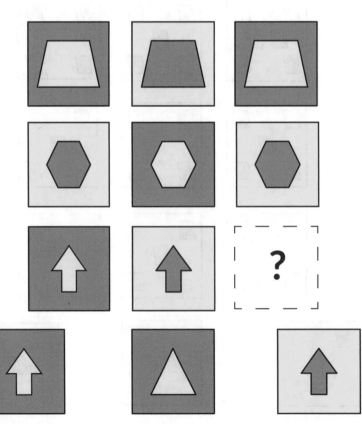

○   ○   ○   ○   ○

39

  ?

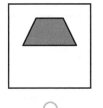   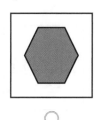 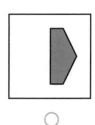

○ ○ ○ ○ ○

40

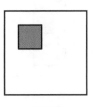 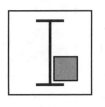 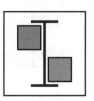

 **?**

 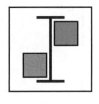 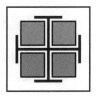

○ ○ ○ ○ ○

41

  ?

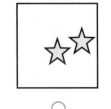    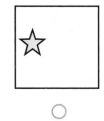

○   ○   ○   ○   ○

42

  ?

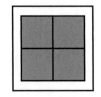  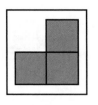 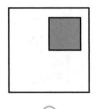 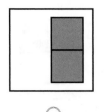

○   ○   ○   ○   ○

43

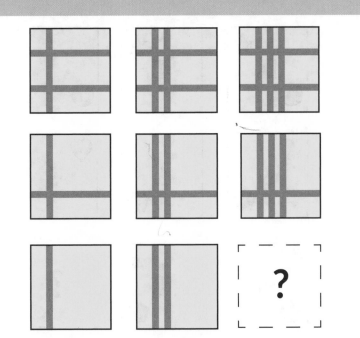

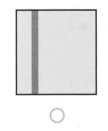

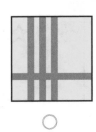

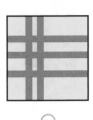

○   ○   ○   ○   ○

44

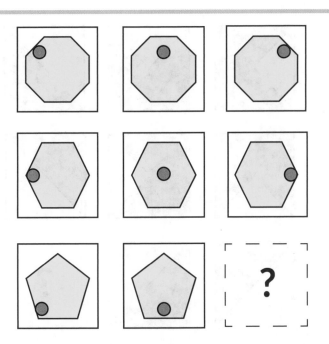

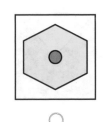

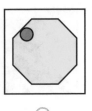

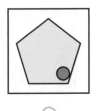

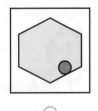

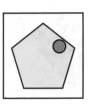

○   ○   ○   ○   ○

45

  ?

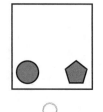 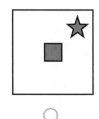 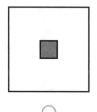  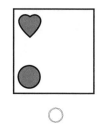

○   ○   ○   ○   ○

46

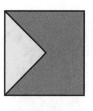  

 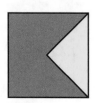

 **?**

   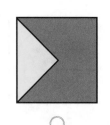 

○   ○   ○   ○   ○

47

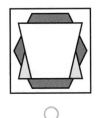 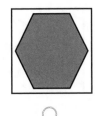  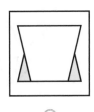 

○ ○ ○ ○ ○

48

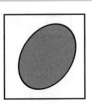 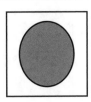 

 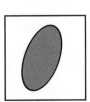

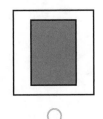 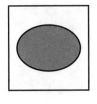 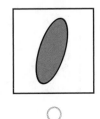  

○ ○ ○ ○ ○

49

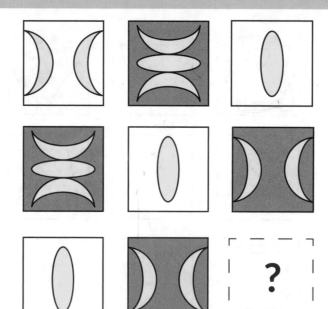

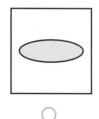 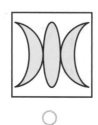 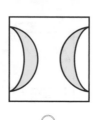 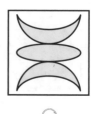

50

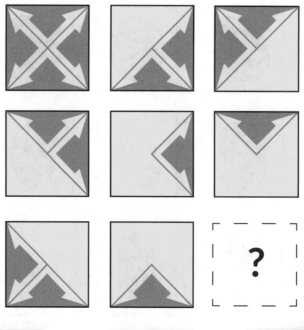

1

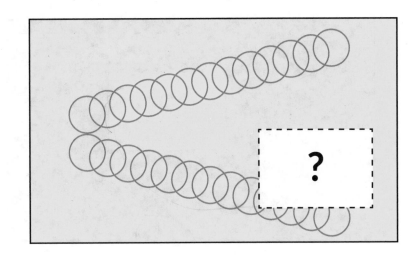

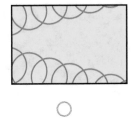  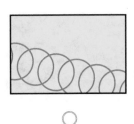 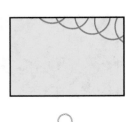 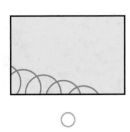

○   ○   ○   ○   ○

2

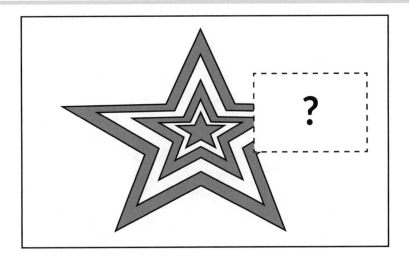

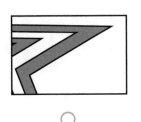 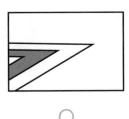 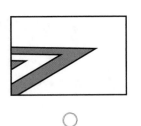 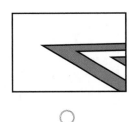 

○   ○   ○   ○   ○

3

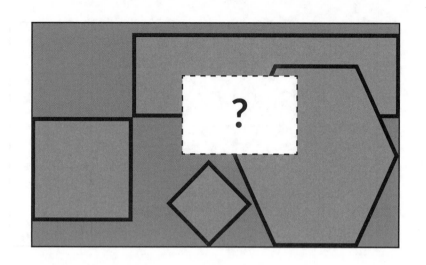

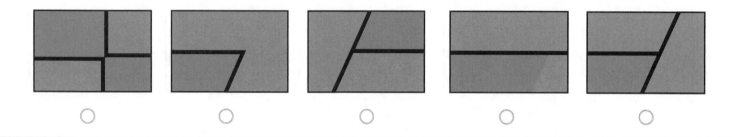

4

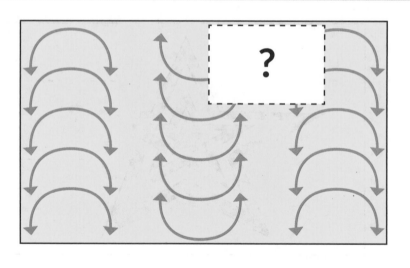

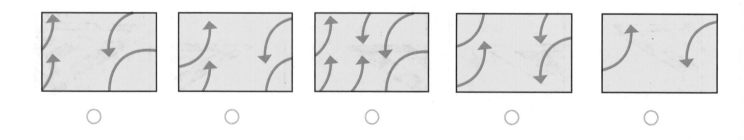

5

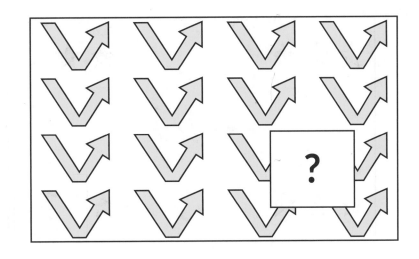

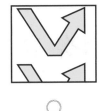   ○

   ○

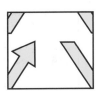   ○

   ○

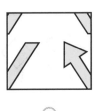   ○

6

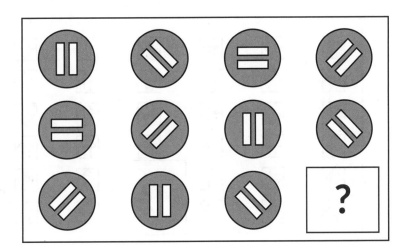

    ○

    ○

    ○

    ○

    ○

7

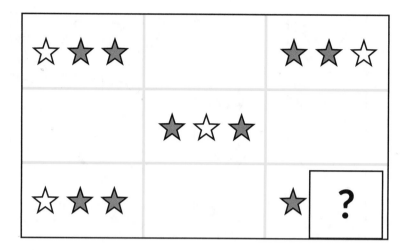

○   ○   ○   ○   ○

8

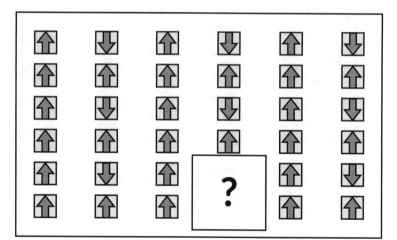

○   ○   ○   ○   ○

9

    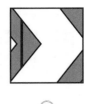

○   ○   ○   ○   ○

10

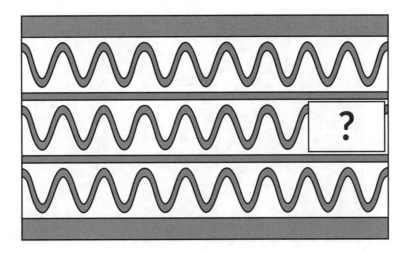

○   ○   ○   ○   ○

11

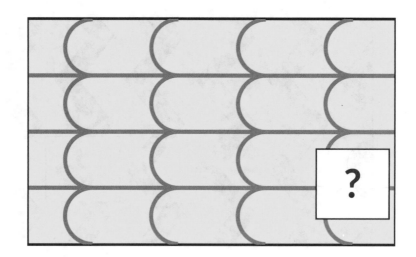

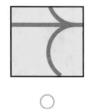

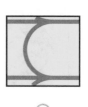

○   ○   ○   ○   ○

12

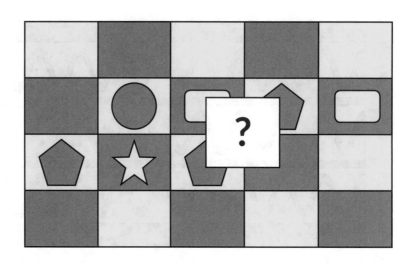

○   ○   ○   ○   ○

13

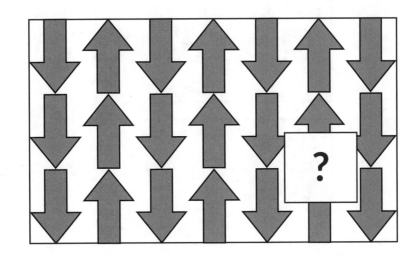

   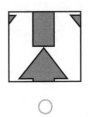

○　　　　○　　　　○　　　　○　　　　○

14

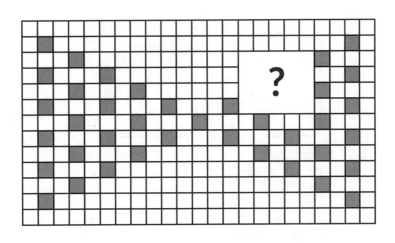

  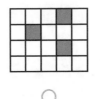 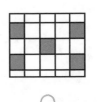

○　　　　○　　　　○　　　　○　　　　○

15

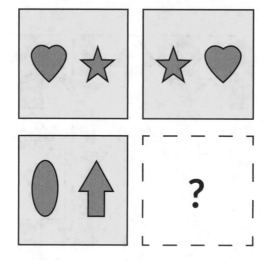

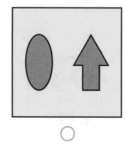

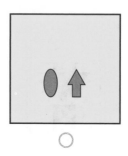

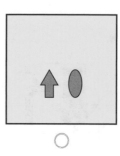

○   ○   ○   ○   ○

16

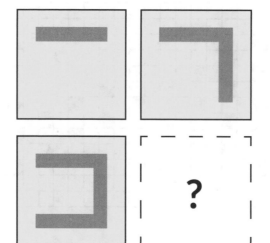

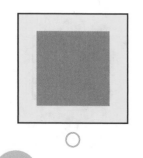

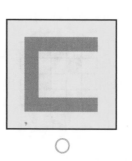

○   ○   ○   ○   ○

17

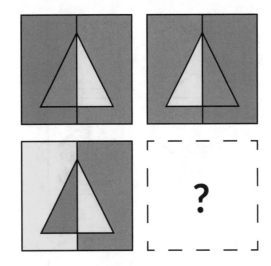

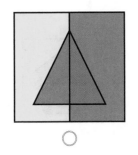
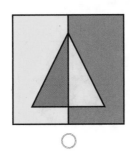
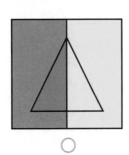

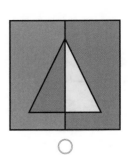

○   ○   ○   ○   ○

18

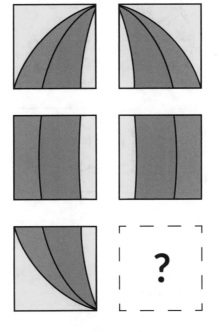

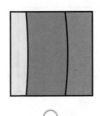

○   ○   ○   ○   ○

19

○

○

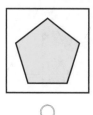
○

○

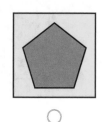
○

20

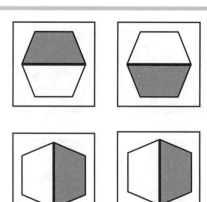

○

○

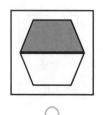
○

○

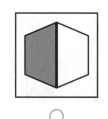
○

21

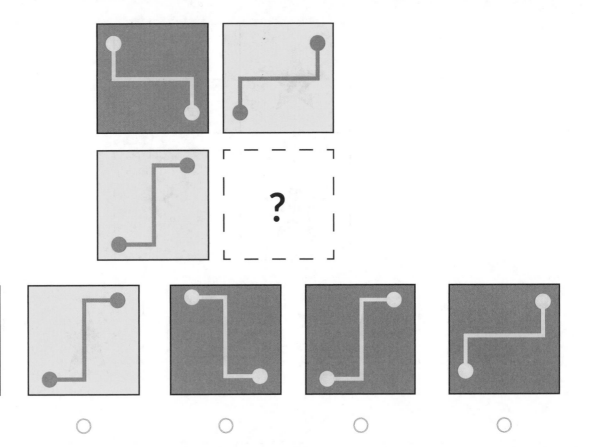

○   ○   ○   ○   ○

22

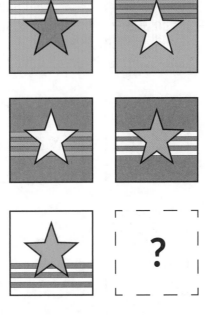

○   ○   ○   ○   ○

23

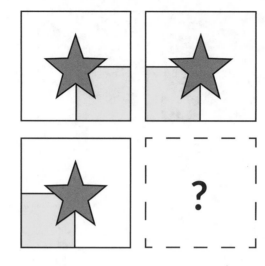

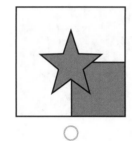

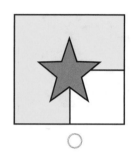

○   ○   ○   ○   ○

24

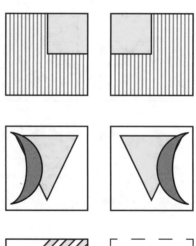

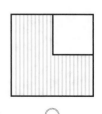

○   ○   ○   ○   ○

25

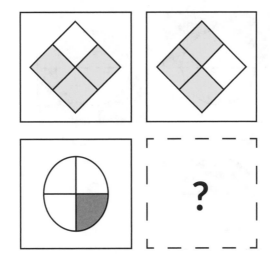

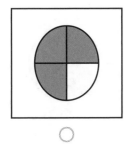
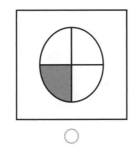
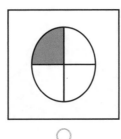
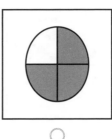
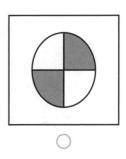

○   ○   ○   ○   ○

26

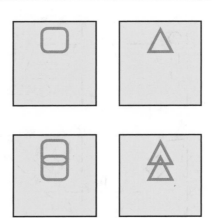

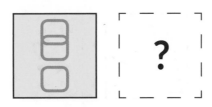

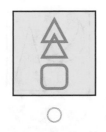
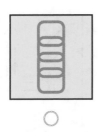

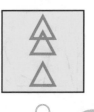

○   ○   ○   ○   ○

27

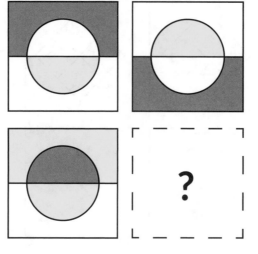

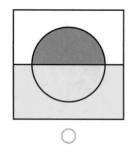 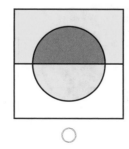 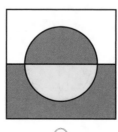 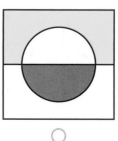 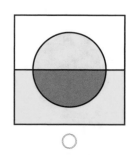

28

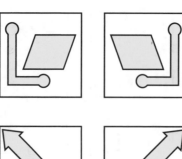

29

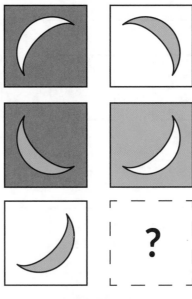

○ ○ ○ ○ ○

30

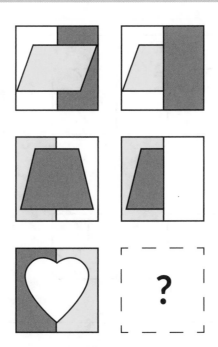

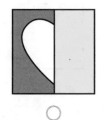 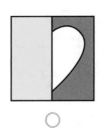  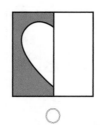 

○ ○ ○ ○ ○

31

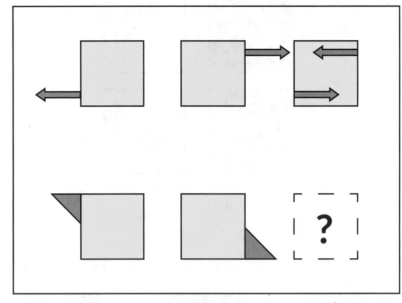

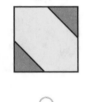   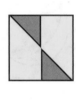

○　　　　○　　　　○　　　　○　　　　○

32

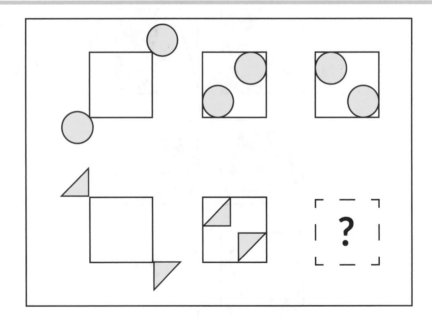

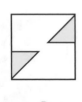 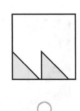 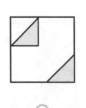 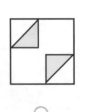 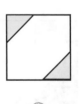

○　　　　○　　　　○　　　　○　　　　○

33

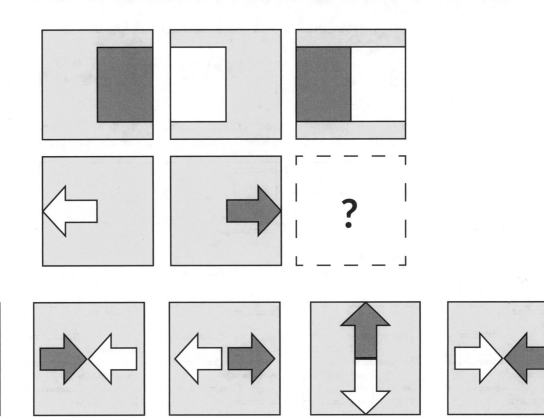

34

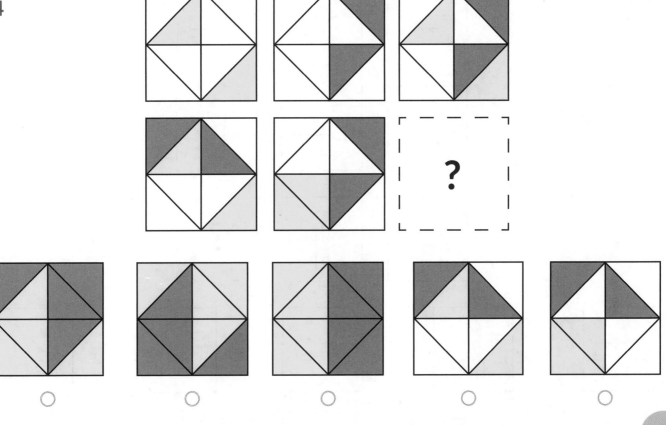

35

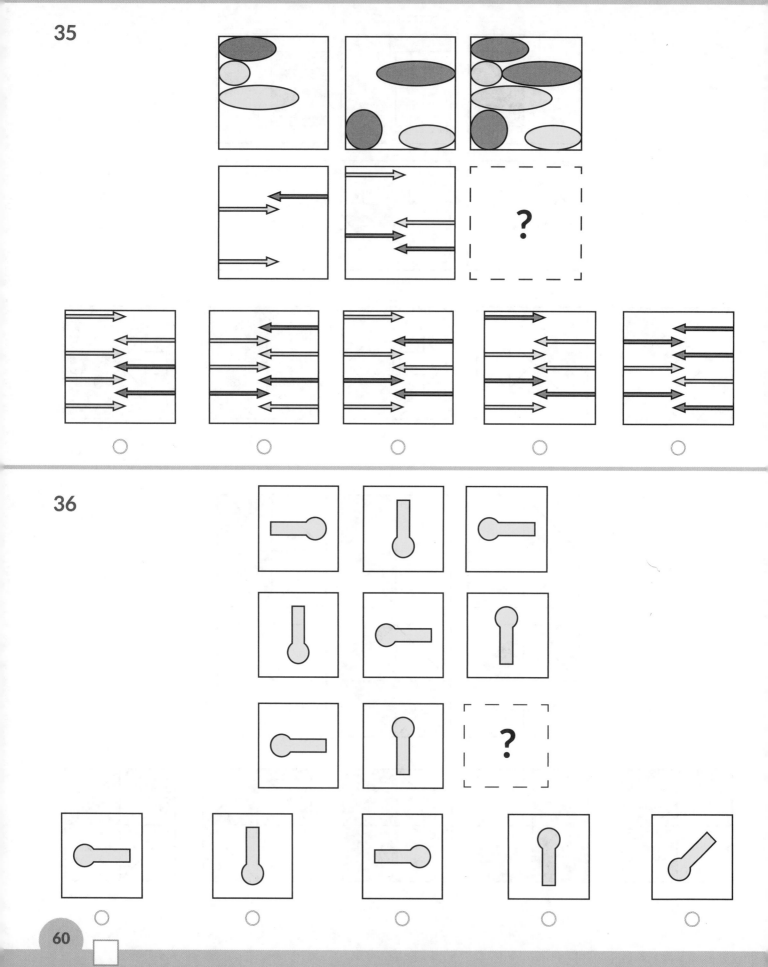

37

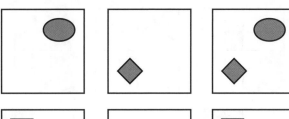

 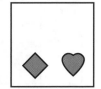 

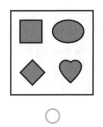 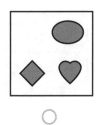 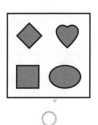 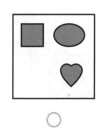 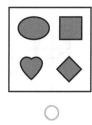

○   ○   ○   ○   ○

38

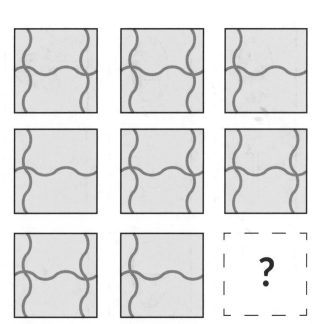

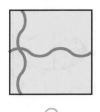 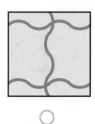 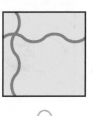 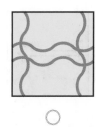 

○   ○   ○   ○   ○

39

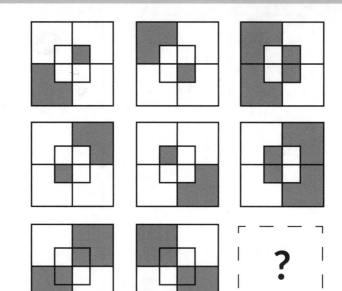

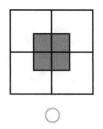 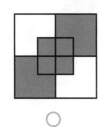 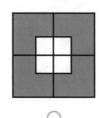 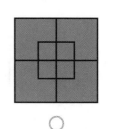 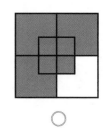

○   ○   ○   ○   ○

40

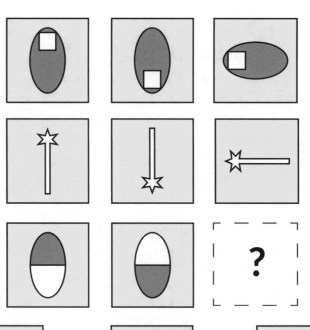

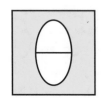  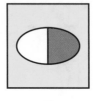 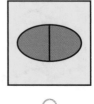 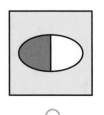

○   ○   ○   ○   ○

41

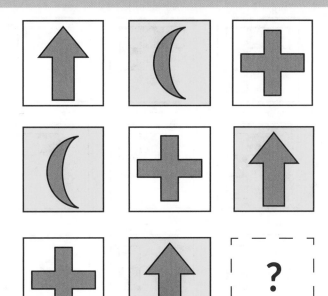

○　　　　○　　　　○　　　　○　　　　○

42

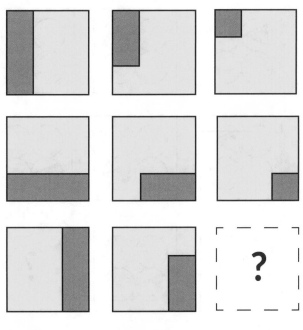

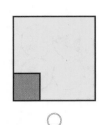
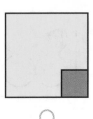

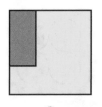

○　　　　○　　　　○　　　　○　　　　○

43

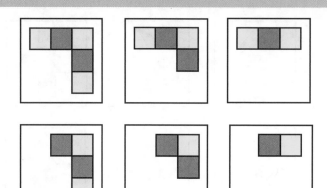

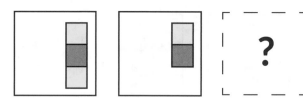

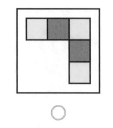
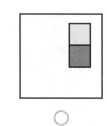
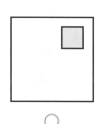
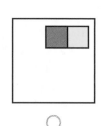
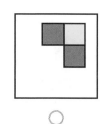

○   ○   ○   ○   ○

44

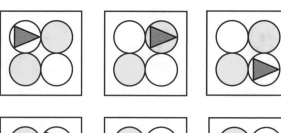

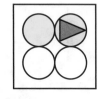
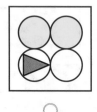
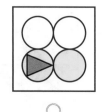
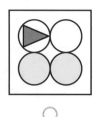
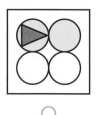

○   ○   ○   ○   ○

45

 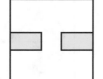

 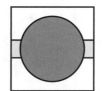 

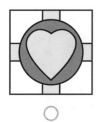 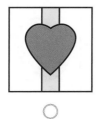  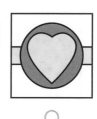 

○   ○   ○   ○   ○

46

  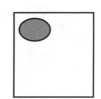

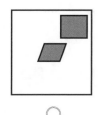  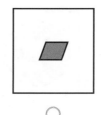 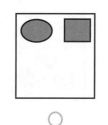 

○   ○   ○   ○   ○

47

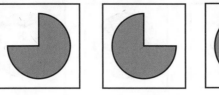

?

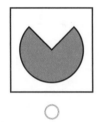

○ ○ ○ ○ ○

48

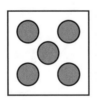

?

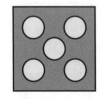
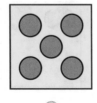
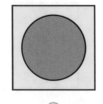
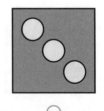
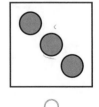

○ ○ ○ ○ ○

49

  ?

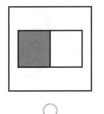 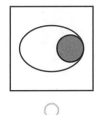 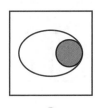 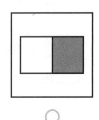 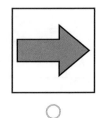

    ○   ○   ○   ○   ○

50

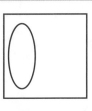 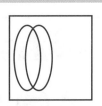

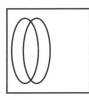 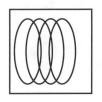

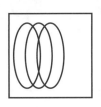 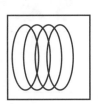 ?

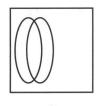 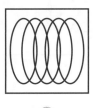 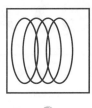 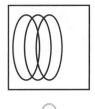 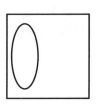

    ○   ○   ○   ○   ○

1

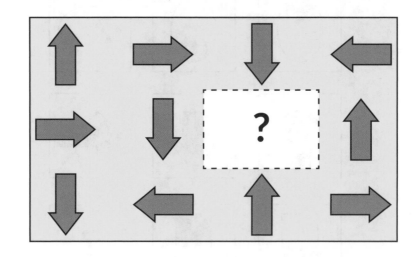

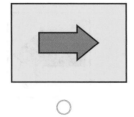   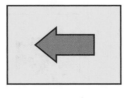   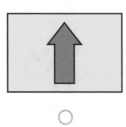   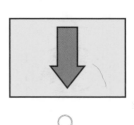   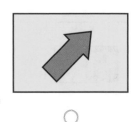

○   ○   ○   ○   ○

2

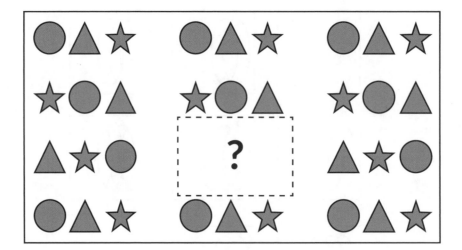

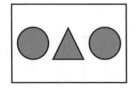            

○   ○   ○   ○   ○

3

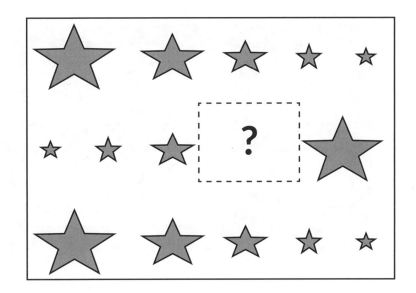

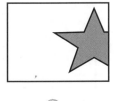   

○   ○   ○   ○   ○

4

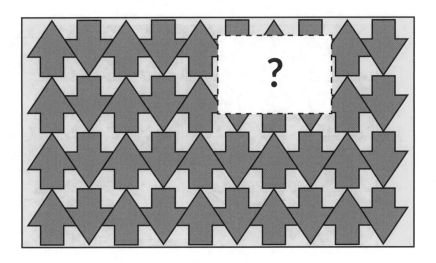

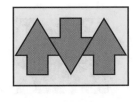 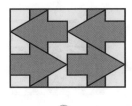 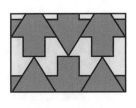 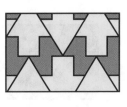 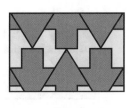

○   ○   ○   ○   ○

5

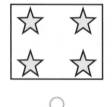    

  ○   ○   ○   ○   ○

6

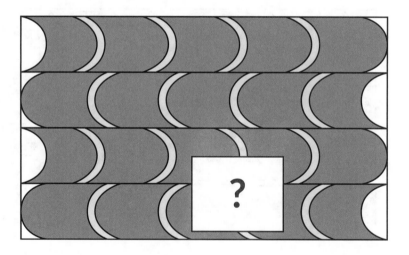

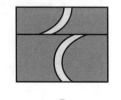 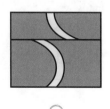 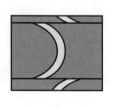 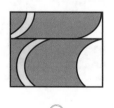 

  ○   ○   ○   ○   ○

7

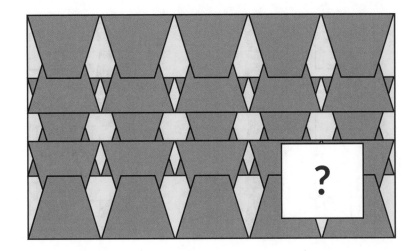

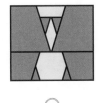 　 　 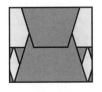 　 　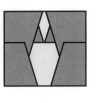

○　　　　　　○　　　　　　○　　　　　　○　　　　　　○

8

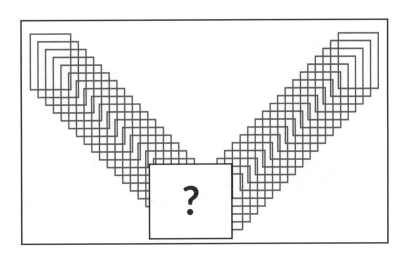

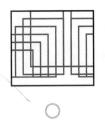 　 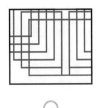 　 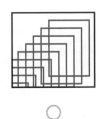 　 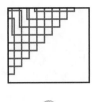 　

○　　　　　　○　　　　　　○　　　　　　○　　　　　　○

9

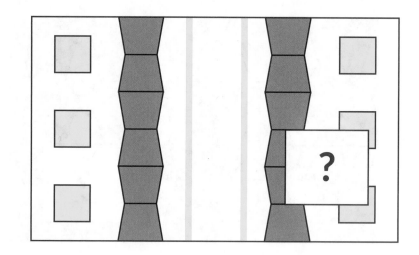

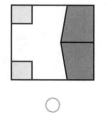 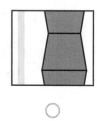 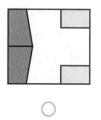 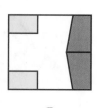 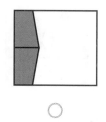

○ ○ ○ ○ ○

10

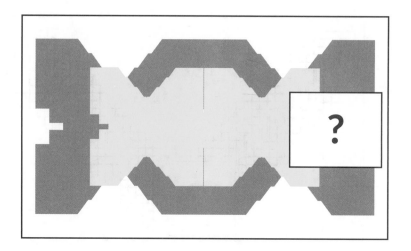

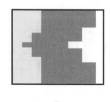 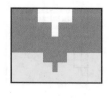  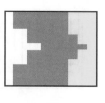 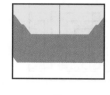

○ ○ ○ ○ ○

11

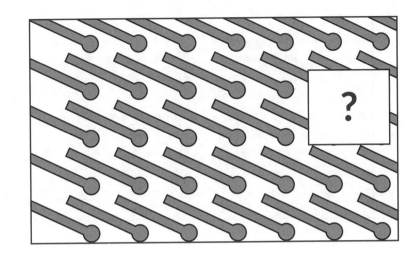

○   ○   ○   ○   ○

12

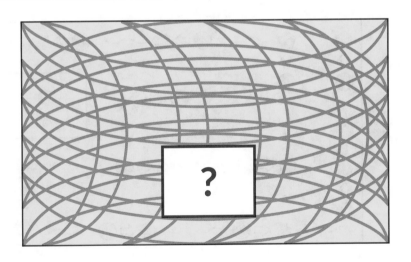

○   ○   ○   ○   ○

13

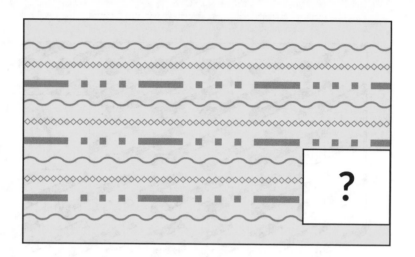

 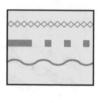 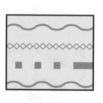 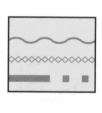 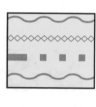

○ ○ ○ ○ ○

14

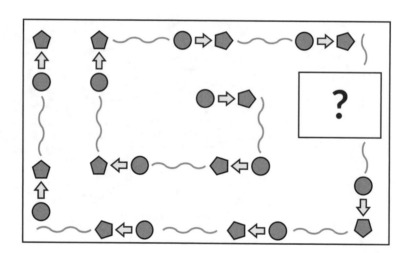

○ ○ ○ ○ ○

15

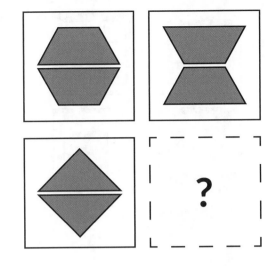

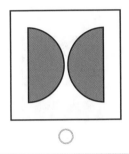 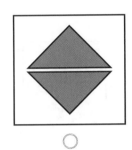 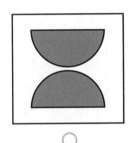 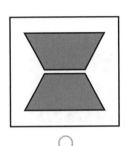 

○ ○ ○ ○ ○

16

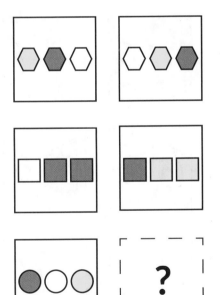

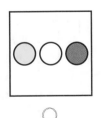 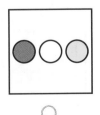 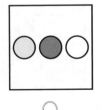 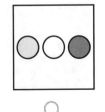

○ ○ ○ ○ ○

17

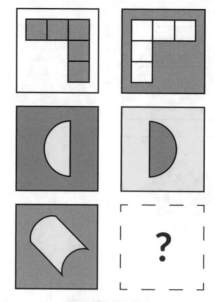

○

○

○

○

○

18

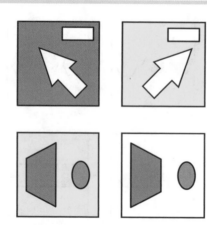

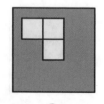
○

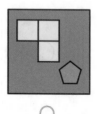
○

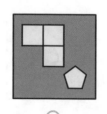
○

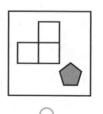
○

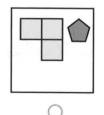
○

19

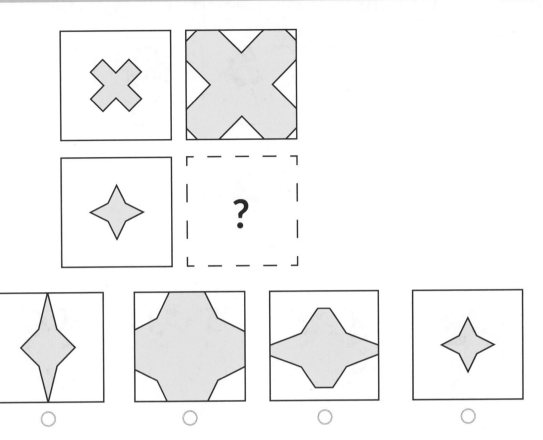

20

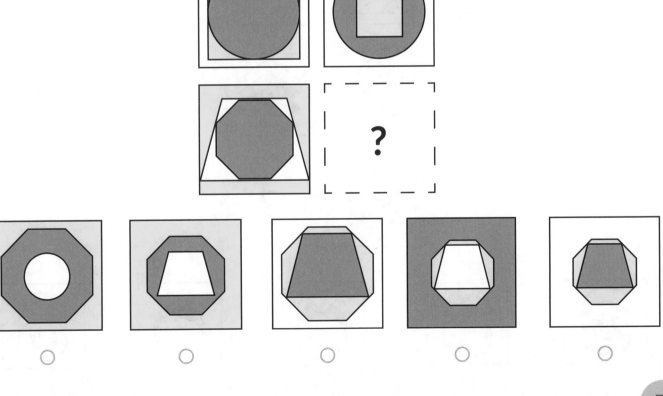

21

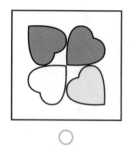 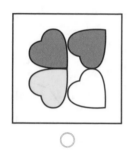 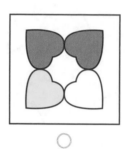 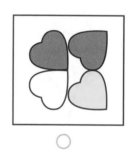 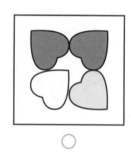

   ○   ○   ○   ○   ○

22

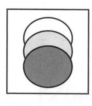

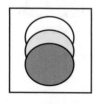 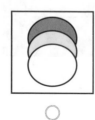 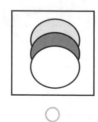  

   ○   ○   ○   ○   ○

23

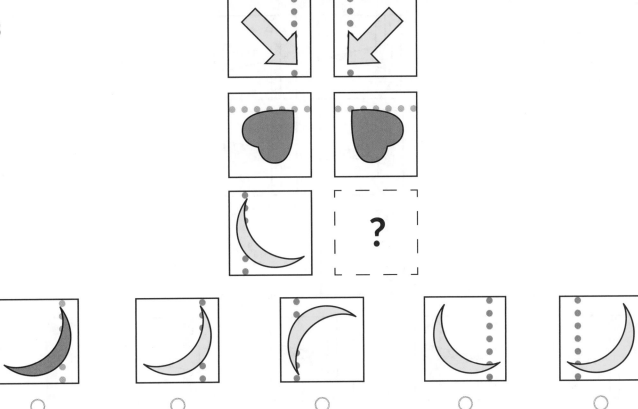

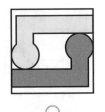  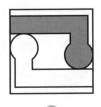 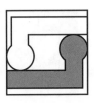 

○ ○ ○ ○ ○

24

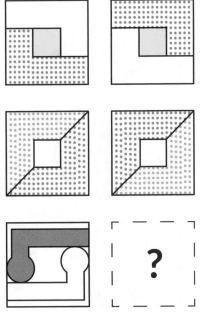

○ ○ ○ ○ ○

25

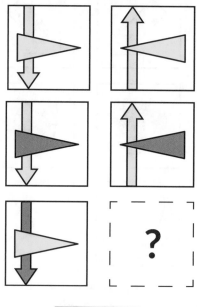

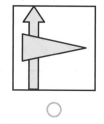   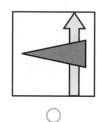   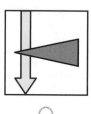   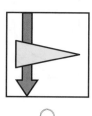   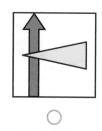

   ○   ○   ○   ○   ○

26

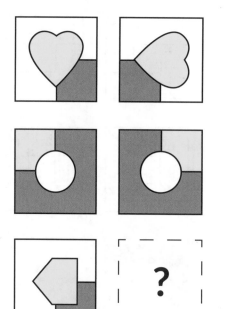

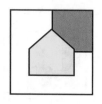   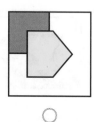   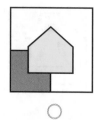   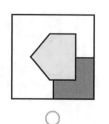   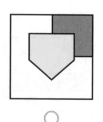

   ○   ○   ○   ○   ○

27

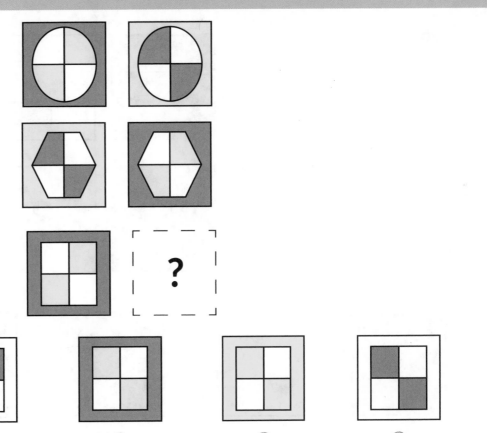

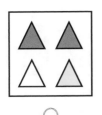 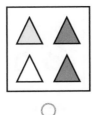 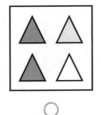 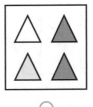

○   ○   ○   ○   ○

28

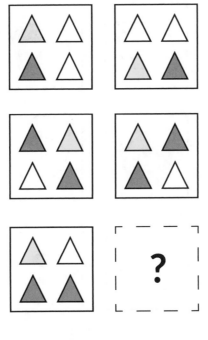

29

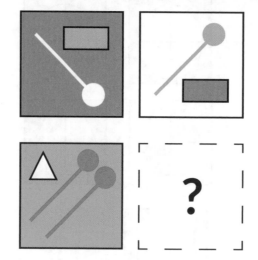

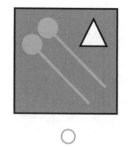   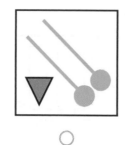      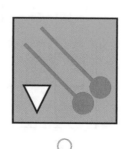   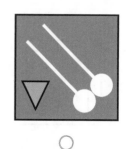

○   ○   ○   ○   ○

30

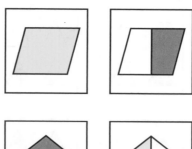

   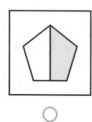   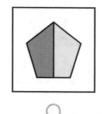      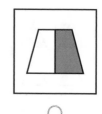

○   ○   ○   ○   ○

31

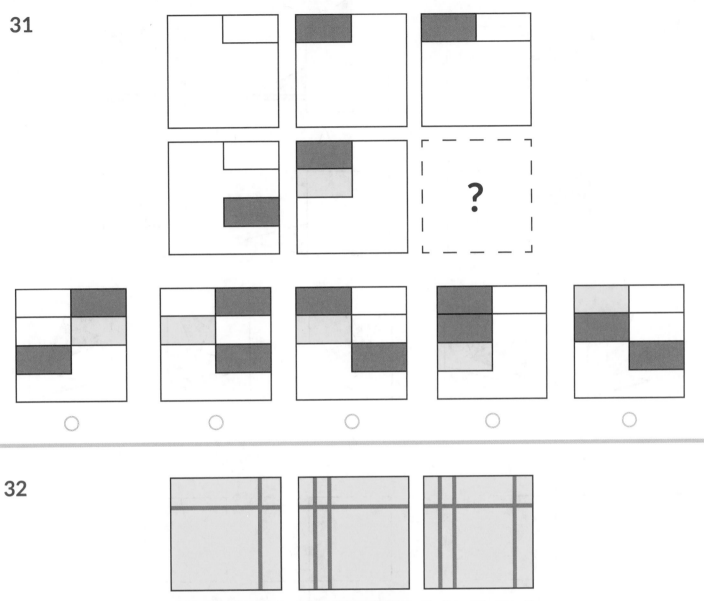

32

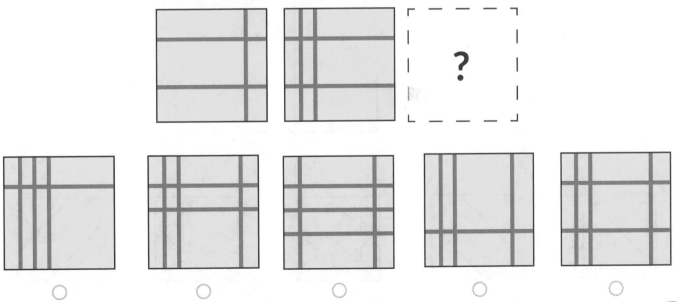

33

34

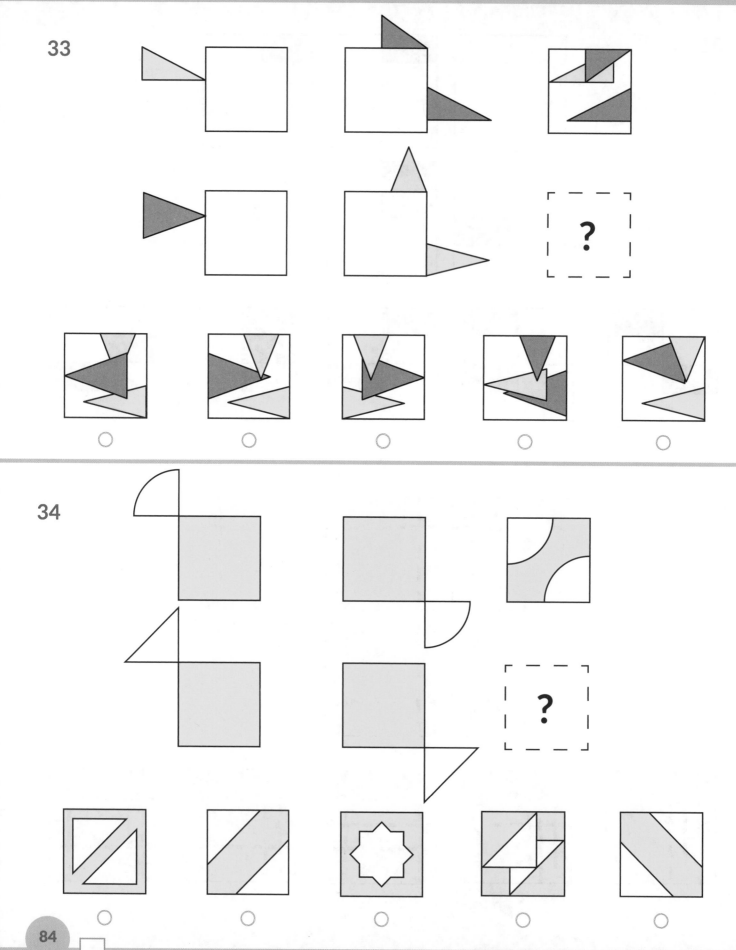

35

36

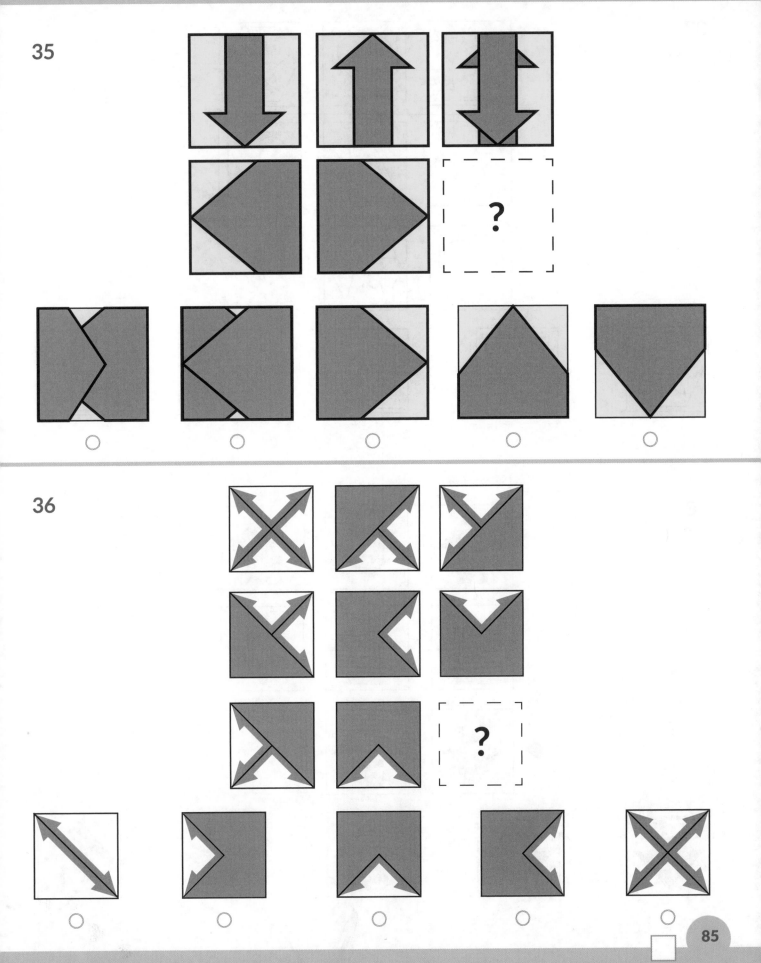

37

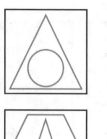 

  ?

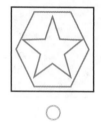    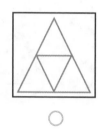

○　　　○　　　○　　　○　　　○

38

 ?

   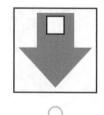 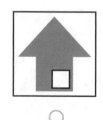

○　　　○　　　○　　　○　　　○

39

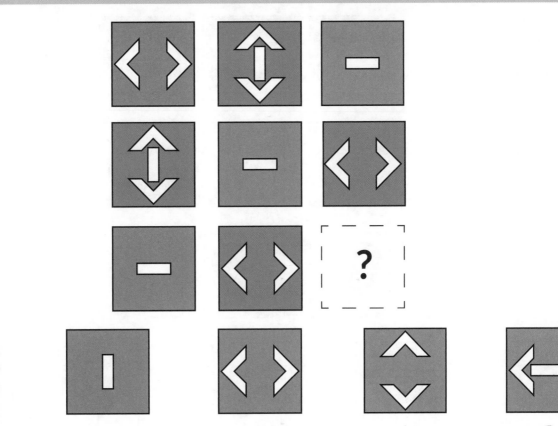

40

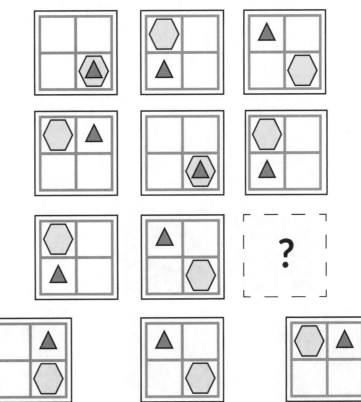

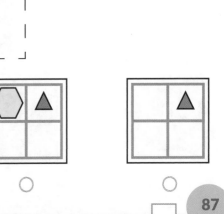

41

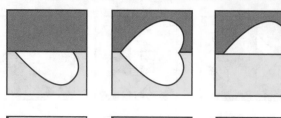

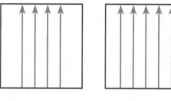 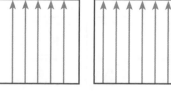 **?**

  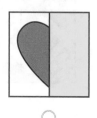 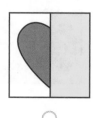 

○ ○ ○ ○ ○

42

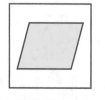 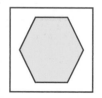

  **?**

○ ○ ○ ○ ○

43

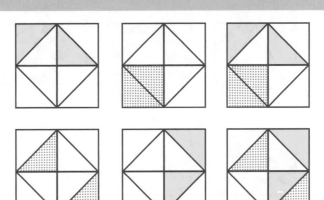

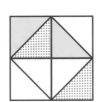 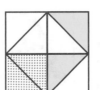

 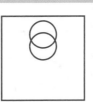 ?

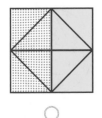 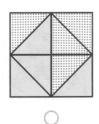 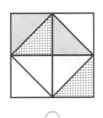 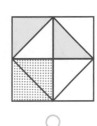 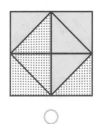

○ ○ ○ ○ ○

44

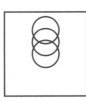 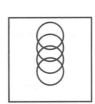 

?

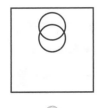 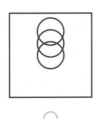 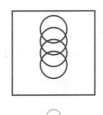 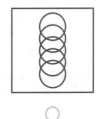 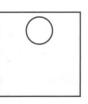

○ ○ ○ ○ ○

45

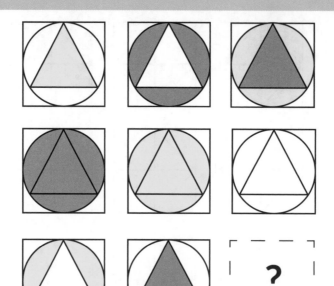

 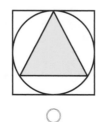  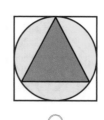 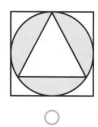

○ ○ ○ ○ ○

46

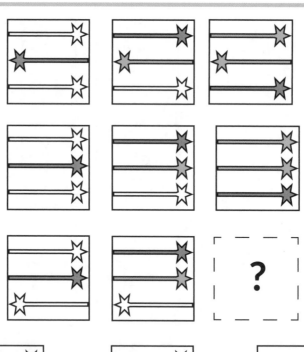

  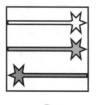  

○ ○ ○ ○ ○

47

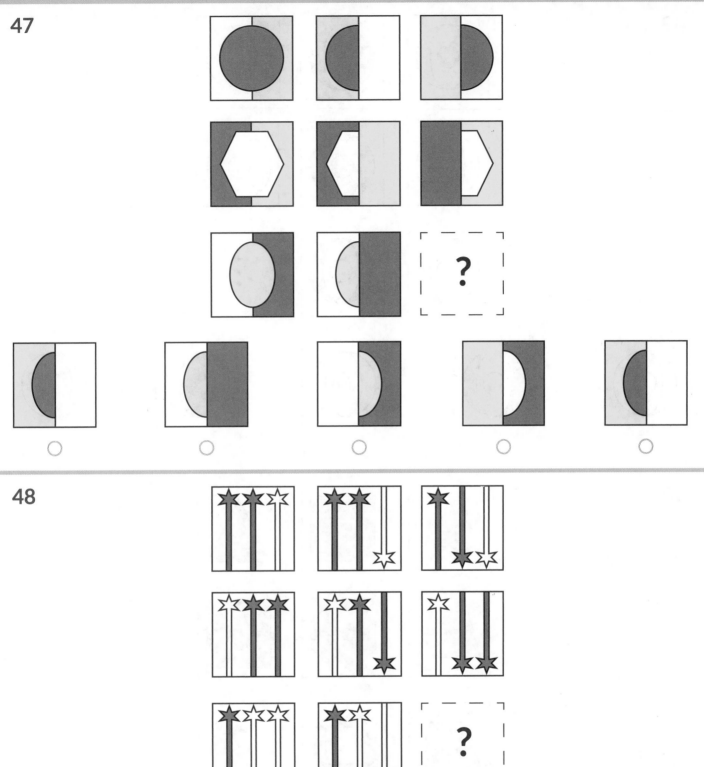

48

49

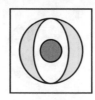

  ?

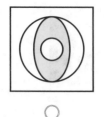  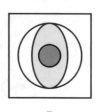 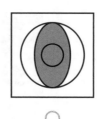 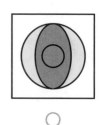

○ ○ ○ ○ ○

50

 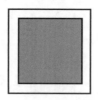 

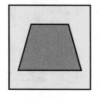

  ?

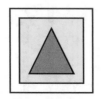   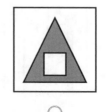 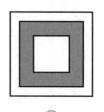

○ ○ ○ ○ ○

IMPORTANT NOTES If you wish to assign a time limit to mimic an actual test, allow approximately 30 minutes per test. Directions for each question type are below in each question type's section. Each of the question types (Pattern Completion, Reasoning by Analogy, Spatial Visualization, Serial Reasoning) have the same directions for each question. Your child should fill in the answer "bubble" below his/her answer. The correct answers are next to the question number. Additional explanations are provided for the Reasoning by Analogy, Spatial Visualization, and Serial Reasoning question types. As most of the Pattern Completion answers are self-explanatory (requiring test-takers to examine the composition of the picture's elements, especially those surrounding the question box), only some of the Pattern Completion questions have additional explanations. At the end of each section, total the number answered correctly. This will give an overview of your child's strengths / challenges relating to question type.

PRACTICE TEST 1, PATTERN COMPLETION, P.18
Directions: Here is a puzzle where a piece is missing. (Point to the box with the question mark.) Which one of the answer choices would go here?

1. D   2. D   3. C   4. E   5. E   6. C   7. B (note shape pattern: triangle-diamond)   8. A   9. D   10. D
11. C (note how arrow rotates 45° counterclockwise as you go across rows, left to right)   12. E   13. E   14. B

Pattern Completion Questions Answered Correctly: _____ out of 14

PRACTICE TEST 1, REASONING BY ANALOGY, P.25
Directions: Look at the pictures inside the boxes on the top row. They go together in some way. On the bottom row, one box is missing. (Point to the question mark.) Look at the answer choices. Which one would go here?

15. B: vertical lines added to square/circle   16. A: shapes switch colors   17. C: gets bigger & becomes blue
18. E: "flips"/becomes mirror image of original   19. C: yellow becomes blue, blue becomes yellow
20. B: "flips" (right box is mirror image of left box)   21. A: triangle rotates to point up; other shape remains the same, in same place
22. D: yellow triangle becomes blue parallelogram & curvy line becomes yellow
23. C: color of triangles & squares switch color   24. E: shape rotates 90° clockwise
25. E: background squares switch color   26. C: shape inside box flips 180° and colors of box/inside shape switch
27. D: blue line moves from behind the yellow shape to the front   28. A: from left to right, a shape having one more side appears
29. B: middle 2 shapes keep same colors (blue & yellow on top; yellow & white on bottom) & the square color changes
30. A: 2 shapes "flip"

Reasoning by Analogy Questions Answered Correctly: _____ out of 16

PRACTICE TEST 1, SPATIAL VISUALIZATION, P.33
Directions: Look at the top row of pictures. The last box shows how the first two pictures would look if they were combined. Look at the bottom row. One box is missing. (Point to the box with a question mark.) Which choice shows how the first two pictures on the bottom would look if they were combined?

31. D   32. B   33. D   34. A   35. B

Spatial Visualization Questions Answered Correctly: _____ out of 5

PRACTICE TEST 1, SERIAL REASONING, P.35
Directions: Look at the pictures inside the boxes. They go together in some way. On the bottom, one box is missing. (Point to the question mark.) Look at the answer choices. Which one would go here?

36. C: across rows & down columns, there is 1 less blue shape
37. C: each row has a yellow heart, diamond, triangle on a green background
38. B: same shape across rows; colors of shape/background switch green/yellow
39. E: whole shape-left half of shape-right half of shape
40. E: across rows and down columns: green & blue squares from 1st & 2nd box combine in last box
41. D: across rows & down columns: 3 stars, 2 stars, 1 star; note position of 2 stars and 1 star in the boxes - on the left; 'A' isn't correct because 2 stars are on the right
42. B: across rows & down columns, there's 1 less blue shape
43. E: across rows, the 3rd box has a combo of lines from the first 2 boxes
44. C: across each row, blue circle moves to right inside same shape
45. E: across rows, 1st box has combo of all shapes that are in 2nd & 3rd boxes, in the same location; the 2nd box has shapes found on right side of 1st box & the 3rd box has shapes found on the left side of the 1st box; down columns, the last box has the combo of the top & middle boxes
46. C: across rows & down columns, last box has combo of yellow shapes in first 2 boxes
47. B: across rows & down columns, middle & last box have the shapes from the first box
48. C: as the shapes go down columns, they get more narrow; each row/column has an oval rotated at an angle, a regular oval, and a shape similar to a rectangle (but with rounded sides)
49. D: each row/column has squares alternating in color white/blue/white (or blue/white/blue), an oval aligned vertically, 2 crescents aligned vertically, and a combo of 2 crescents with an oval aligned horizontally
50. E: the first box in the row/column shows the object with the most blue parts; the next two boxes each show approximately half of the first box's blue part

Serial Reasoning Questions Answered Correctly: _____ out of 15

PRACTICE TEST 2, PATTERN COMPLETION, P.43
Directions: Here is a puzzle where a piece is missing. (Point to the box with the question mark.) Which one of the answer choices would go here?

1. E   2. C   3. E   4. B   5. D   6. E (object rotates 45° across rows)   7. C (note color of stars in upper right)
8. E (note arrow pattern in this column; down, up, down, etc.)   9. A   10. B   11. C   12. E   13. D   14. B

Pattern Completion Questions Answered Correctly: _____ out of 14

PRACTICE TEST 2, REASONING BY ANALOGY, P.50
Directions: Look at the pictures inside the top boxes. They go together in some way. On the bottom row, one box is missing. (Point to the question mark.) Look at the answer choices. Which one would go here?

15. E: shapes switch position
16. D: 1 more blue bar added around inner square
17. D: square halves switch color & triangle halves switch color
18: E: square flips/becomes mirror image
19. C: star changes to pentagon, colors remain same
20. B: inner shape "flips" vertically (note that in the middle 2 you don't notice the vertical flip, so it looks the same)
21. C: figure "flips" horizontally & colors switch
22. D: colors of stars & lines switch
23. A: "flips" horizontally
24. D: "flips" horizontally
25. B: the shapes are divided into quarters; 3/4 is one color, 1/4 is a different color; the "quarters" rotate 1/4 clockwise; i.e., on top, the white quarter of the diamond rotates clockwise from top "quarter" to right "quarter"
26. E: in the left boxes are squares with rounded corners, in the right boxes are triangles; the quantity & position of the rounded corner squares equals that of the triangles
27. E: the squares are divided in half & the circles are divided in half; from left to right, the square halves switch colors & the circle halves switch colors
28. C: "flips" horizontally
29. B: the crescent "flips"; the color of the crescent will be the color that does not appear in the original box or the original crescent; the color of the box is the color of the original crescent; using the top set as an example: on the left, the top crescent is white, so the top right box will be white; the color that is not in the top left set is yellow, so the top right crescent is yellow
30. A: right side of the first box covers up the right side of shape

Reasoning by Analogy Questions Answered Correctly: _____ out of 16

PRACTICE TEST 2, SPATIAL VISUALIZATION, P.58
Directions: Look at the top row of pictures. The last box shows how the first two pictures would look if they were combined. On the bottom row, one box is missing. (Point to the bottom box that has a question mark.) Which answer choice shows how the first two pictures on the bottom row would look when combined?

31. D: note that the outer blue shapes "flip in" to the yellow box
32. A: shapes outside square go inside & move to opposite corners (right moves to left; left moves to right)
33: B: blue & white shapes are combined in the final box and have switched order so that blue shape is first
34. A: colors of triangles in first 2 boxes are combined in last box   35. C: shapes from first two boxes are all found in the last box

Spatial Visualization Questions Answered Correctly: _____ out of 5

PRACTICE TEST 2, SERIAL REASONING, P.60
Directions: Look at these pictures inside the boxes. They go together in some way. On the bottom, one box is missing. (Point to the question mark.) Look at the answer choices. Which one would go here?

36. C: across rows & down columns, shape rotates 90° clockwise
37. A: across rows & down columns, shapes in 1st & 2nd box combine in last box
38. E: across rows & down columns are 2 boxes with 1 vertical line on left, 1 vertical line on right, 1 horizontal line in middle -and- 1 box with 1 vertical line on the left, 1 horizontal line in middle; lines are all green curvy lines
39. D: across rows & down columns, the green squares from the 1st and 2nd box combine in the 3rd
40. E: across rows, shape rotates like this - 2nd box: 180°, 3rd box: 90° clockwise
41. C: in rows/columns: color pattern of squares is white/yellow/white (or, yellow/white/yellow) & there's 1 each of these shapes: arrow, crescent, cross
42. B: across rows, blue bar decreases each time (and stays on same side)
43. C: across rows & down columns: minus 1 square each time
44. E: across rows, blue triangle moves clockwise once around group of circles
45. A: last box in each row is a combo of the elements in the 1st 2 boxes; shapes from 1st 2 boxes combine in last box in each column
46. B: across rows, 3rd box & 2nd box have shapes that combine to make the 1st box (in same position); down columns, 1st box & 2nd box have shapes that combine to make the 3rd box   47. E: figure rotates 90° clockwise across rows
48. D: across rows/down columns, there must be 1 box of each color (yellow/white/blue) and there must be 1 box with 1 large circle, 3 small circles, 5 small circles   49. D: across rows, figure rotates 180° & then 90° clockwise
50. B: across rows/down columns: +1 large oval

Serial Reasoning Questions Answered Correctly: _____ out of 15

PRACTICE TEST 3, PATTERN COMPLETION, P.68
Directions: Here is a puzzle where a piece is missing. (Point to the box with the question mark.) Which one of the answer choices would go here?

1. B   2. D (each group of 3 shapes across the row repeats)   3. E (note size change of stars across the 3 rows)   4. E
5. D (-1 star in rows / columns; box is same color)   6. A   7. E   8. B   9. C   10. A   11. E   12. D
13. C (note the series of 3 small squares & 1 rectangle)
14. B (note pattern of blue pentagon/yellow arrow/blue circle stays the same as they travel along the wavy line; under the white box, it would be pointing down)

Pattern Completion Questions Answered Correctly: _____ out of 14

PRACTICE TEST 3, REASONING BY ANALOGY, P.75
Directions: Look at the pictures inside the boxes on the top row. They go together in some way. On the bottom row, one box is missing. (Point to the question mark.) Look at the answer choices. Which one would go here?

15. E: 2 shape halves rotate 180°

16. C: green>yellow, white>green, yellow>white

17. A: shape "flips" & colors switch

18. B: box color must change, larger inside shape flips, smaller inside shape stays same color/in same place

19. C: original shape enlarges so all the endpoints can not be seen

20. B: in the group of 2 shapes in middle (yellow square & blue circle on top; white trapezoid & blue octagon on bottom), outer shape becomes smaller and moves to the middle of the inner shape (note the color of the shapes remains the same)

21. D: group of hearts "flips" (note that in the bottom box, when you flip the 2 hearts on the right, choice D is the only choice with the blue heart & white heart flipped correctly)

22. E: blue becomes yellow, white becomes blue, yellow becomes white

23. B: the large shape and dotted line "flip" horizontally

24. D: the 2 larger figures inside the square switch colors

25. E: arrow points up & triangle "flips" horizontally

26. C: rotation of 90° clockwise (in middle set, you don't notice the 90° rotation because it's a circle; in top set, you can see this)

27. A: object inside square "flips" horizontally & the colors of the square and the sections of the shape inside the square switch yellow to blue & blue to yellow

28. D: the group of triangles with colors moves 1 triangle counter-clockwise around the group of 4 triangles

29. E: shape "flips" vertically & blue becomes white, white becomes yellow, yellow becomes blue

30. D: same object as first box, but divided in half and both halves are a different color than the original shape

Reasoning by Analogy Questions Answered Correctly: _____ out of 16

PRACTICE TEST 3, SPATIAL VISUALIZATION, P.83
Directions: Look at the top row of pictures. The last box shows how the first two pictures would look if they were combined. Look at the bottom row. One box is missing. (Point to the bottom box that has a question mark.) Which answer choice shows how the first two pictures on the bottom row would look when combined?

31. C

32. E

33. E: the 3 shapes "flip in" to the white box; triangle on top side of square goes over triangle on the left side

34. B: the shapes outside the yellow square "flip in" to the yellow square.

35. B: the 1st shape is on top of the 2nd shape (blue shape from the 1st box must be on top of blue shape from the 2nd box)

Spatial Visualization Questions Answered Correctly: _____ out of 5

PRACTICE TEST 3, SERIAL REASONING, P.85
Directions: Look at the pictures inside the boxes. They go together in some way. On the bottom, one box is missing. Look at the answer choices. Which one would go in the box with the question mark?

36. B: the white sections in the 2nd and 3rd boxes in the rows/columns equal the white sections in the 1st box

37. C: each row/column has same 3 groups of same 2 shapes

38. E: each row/column has an empty green arrow, a green arrow with white circle, and a green arrow with white square in corner; 2 arrows face up, 1 arrow faces down

39. A: each row/column has 1 box with 1 vertically-aligned white, double-sided arrow, 1 box with 2 horizontally-aligned arrow points, 1 box with 1 horizontally-aligned middle section of arrow; 1 box is green and 2 are blue

40. D: across rows: inside the square sections, the green triangle moves around clockwise & yellow hexagon changes position in 2nd box, but in 3rd box it returns to its original position

41. B: each row has 1 full heart showing, 1 half of heart showing, the other half of heart showing; color of box halves remain the same

42. C: across the rows, the concept is "+1" (+1: arrows, number of shape sides, number of star points); down the columns the concept, when looking at arrows/shape sides/star points, is "4" in column 1, "5" in column 2, and "6" in column 3

43. E: across rows/down columns, the filled in sections from the first 2 boxes equal the filled in sections in the last box

44. D: across rows/down columns, 1 more circle is added

45. A: across rows/down columns are 1 circle & 1 triangle of each color (yellow/white/blue)

46. A: across rows, the "wands" point the same direction (i.e., in the top row, they point: right, left, right) & down the columns they are the same color (i.e. in the first column, the colors are white, blue, white), so the last box's colors must be yellow, yellow, blue and the "wands" must point right, right, left because across the first 2 boxes in the last row they point right, right, left

47. C: across rows, pattern is full shape showing, left half showing, right half showing; the colors stay the same across the rows

48. A: across rows, 1st wand on the right rotates 90° (or, points down), then the middle wand rotates 90°

49. D: the figures inside the white boxes are groups of 3 shapes (a circle, an oval, and a smaller circle); across the rows, each 1 of these shapes will have a color; across the rows, there will be 1 of each kind of shape that's blue/yellow/white

50. C: across rows, the boxes have the same color scheme (blue in first row, blue with yellow background in second row, and blue shape with smaller yellow shape inside for the last row); also, down the columns, the shape in the middle row is the same as the bottom box and the shape in the top box becomes smaller, turns yellow, and is inside the shape in the bottom box

Serial Reasoning Questions Answered Correctly: _____ out of 15

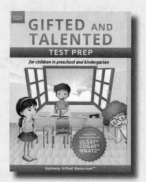
Did your child finish the exercises? Here's a certificate for your new detective! (Please cut along the dotted lines.)

The Kids' Detective Agency

Congratulations to:

_____

Our Newest Member!